BUCKMAN

THE MAN FOR OTHERS

The Man for Others

BY

ERIK ROUTLEY

44820

An important contribution to the
discussions inspired by the book
Honest to God

NEW YORK
OXFORD UNIVERSITY PRESS
1964

Contents

GOOD FRIDAY

It was on a Friday morning that they took me from the cell,
And I saw they had a carpenter to crucify as well.
You can blame it on to Pilate, you can blame it on the Jews,
You can blame it on the Devil, but it's God I accuse.
　　"It's God they ought to crucify instead of you and me,"
　　I said to the carpenter a-hanging on the tree.

You can blame it on to Adam, you can blame it on to Eve.
You can blame it on the apple (but that I don't believe).
It was God that made the Devil, and the woman and the man,
And there wouldn't be an apple if it wasn't in the plan.
　　"It's God they ought to crucify instead of you and me,"
　　I said to the carpenter a-hanging on the tree.

Now Barabbas was a killer, and they let Barabbas go,
But you are being crucified for nothing here below.
And God is up in heaven, but he doesn't do a thing;
With a million angels watching, and they never move a wing.
　　"It's God they ought to crucify instead of you and me,"
　　I said to the carpenter a-hanging on the tree.

"To Hell with Jehovah!" to the carpenter I said,
"I wish that a carpenter had made the world instead.
Good-bye, and good luck to you; our ways they will divide:
Remember me in heaven, the man you hung beside—
　　"It's God they ought to crucify instead of you and me,"
　　I said to the carpenter a-hanging on the tree.

SYDNEY CARTER

Introduction

"THE Man for Others" is the heading of chapter four in the now famous book, *Honest to God*, by Dr J. A. T. Robinson, Bishop of Woolwich. The expression is formed by abridging a phrase in Dietrich Bonhoeffer's *Letters and Papers from Prison*, which in English reads: "man existing for others, hence the Crucified". The four words I have taken for the title of this book, then, represent in a convenient epigram the Christology which Bonhoeffer and Robinson suggest in their writings.[1]

The purpose of the following pages is to pursue some thoughts on Christology which are suggested by those words. Let it be at once stated that I would not claim one hundredth part either of the learning of the Bishop of Woolwich or of the rich Christian insight of Bonhoeffer; indeed I am far from being an authority on the written works of either. But two things moved me to enter upon the present business. The first was a conviction I have long held that a restatement of Christology was overdue; the second was the fact that what Dr Robinson writes in that fourth chapter seemed to me to be exactly what I was looking for to bring my own thoughts into some kind of order. Dr Robinson describes the Bonhoeffer corpus of writings somewhere as "tantalizing intimations" of a theology that Bonhoeffer never had time to work out in writing. I am venturing to treat the paragraph which begins half way down page 74 of *Honest to God* and ends half way down the following page similarly as a "tantalizing intimation".

I have publicly expressed my admiration of and gratitude for *Honest to God*. I still feel that on balance it will be found to have fertilized the church's thinking far beyond any temporary confusion or perplexity its teaching may have caused. I have

[1] J. A. T. Robinson, *Honest to God* (SCM 1963) pp. 64, 74; D. Bonhoeffer, *Letters and Papers from Prison* (SCM 1953) p. 179.

also, in print, ventured to ask what I believe to be a radical question about its axioms concerning "images"—a matter which is entirely beside the point I hope here to pursue. Its author is the chief of those who believe that *Honest to God* says a first word rather than a last word on the subjects it is handling. I am, anyhow, of those who see in it matter for great thanksgiving.

In the following pages the book will here and there be referred to. One thing that I think needs to be made quite clear is that the conclusions towards which that book are leading are wholly supported by the spirit of Scripture. The more I come to grips with *Honest to God* the more Biblical I believe it to be: and of course anybody who thinks otherwise must be reckoning without the high standing of its author in New Testament scholarship.

I shall not here be quoting from a literature as wide as that which the Bishop appeals to. I shall be quoting much more from Scripture. In my pursuit of a Christology I do not find that the end of the story tells us anything new. What I hope is that it interprets what the Scriptures offer, and what the Church in its classic days took for its doctrine. I do think that popular religion (which is all that the ordinary man ever has any patience with) tends towards a pernicious distortion of the truth about Christology. But I do not find that we have to strain the Scriptures, or even to repudiate the old definitions of the Church, in order to make practical sense of the Christological doctrines we claim to hold.

One thing I wish to say before I begin. Dr Robinson very fully acknowledges his debt to Bonhoeffer, and to Tillich, and to John Wren-Lewis. But I fancy that the question he raises near the beginning of his book is not as new a question as these acknowledgments imply. Bonhoeffer's *Letters and Papers* appeared in 1953 in the English edition; the same year saw the publication of Tillich's *Systematic Theology* (volume I). It is during the decade between that year and the present that this particular theological controversy has boiled up. But I really must point out that the paradoxical antithesis between "religion" and "Christianity", of which much is made in the opening pages of *Honest to God*, was stated, and handled with ruthless clarity, in the work of an author whom Dr Robinson mentions but once, and that with scant approval. C. S. Lewis who is dismissed in a line on page 15, stated the problem in chapter XI of his *Miracles* (Bles, 1947). His purpose was not the same as Dr Robinson's, neither were his conclusions: but there is a strange antipathy to his work among those who are most notably in support of what one could compendiously call the *Honest to God* theology, and I for one wish to record that I see no reason for this.[1]

Mention of another author of whom Dr Robinson might well have taken greater notice in support of his scepticism of popular formulae will move us nearer to the point of the present book. Dr Nathaniel Micklem in the Cole Lectures at Vanderbilt University, U.S.A., delivered in 1954 and published in 1955 as *Ultimate Questions*, wrote: "Although in principle the Church has always maintained that Christ was Very Man as well as Very God, yet in fact his alleged humanity has been swallowed up in his divinity in traditional Christian thinking".[2] This seems to agree with what the Bishop writes on p. 65 of his book about the two Natures in Christ: "To use an analogy, if one has to present the doctrine of the person of Christ as a union of oil and water, then the early Church made the best possible attempt to do so. . . . But it is not surprising that in popular Christianity the oil and water separated, and that one or other came to the top." In what one could call popular orthodoxy it was, says Dr Micklem, the Divine Nature. (When oil and water are in question, there is no doubt which will come to the top.) Traditionally an over-emphasis on the Humanity has always tended to lead to positions that the Church labelled as eccentric: an over-emphasis on the Divinity has led to positions which were comfortably accommodated within orthodoxy.

[1] C. S. Lewis, *Miracles*: see especially pp. 106–7. Professor Lewis wrote somewhat impatiently of *Honest to God* in a symposium of reviews in the *Sunday Times* (March 24, 1963); not, I thought, without justice.
[2] N. Micklem, *Ultimate Questions* (Bles, 1955) p. 65.

The question I propose to put here—and I hope to find my answers in the New Testament—is whether we do not stand in considerable danger at present in consequence of a certain error in our approach to the Christ whom the New Testament presents to us. We have a doctrine, given to us by the Church on its reading of the New Testament. But as Dr Micklem says, "If we read the Scriptures on the assumption that He was the God-man, or God and man in one, or both Son of God and Son of Man, we shall think we understand; but do we know what our words mean?"[1] I believe that we are in constant danger in our popular orthodoxy of paying to Jesus a regard which he expressly stated that he does not want, and of withholding the honour which he does demand.

I want then—taking a position which is by no means on all fours with that of the *Honest to God* school, but in which I acknowledge that I owe them much—to examine what possibilities there are of translating into terms of worship and practical life the truth about the two natures of Christ, and the Gospel of reconciliation which he came to body forth among us. To this end, I wish to begin with our human predicament, and the best illustration we can find of this is in the Book of Job.

[1] N. Micklem, *op. cit.*, p. 66.

THE MAN FOR OTHERS

CHAPTER I

Vindicator or Redeemer?

Faith in John Doe

IF an ordinary man wishes to give content to the familiar words "reconciliation" and "faith", he is obliged to begin his understanding of them by referring to his ordinary experience. Even if he wishes to apply these words to the divine order in the end, he has no choice but to start from where he himself stands. He cannot begin his human life in the New Testament; he is born into it "not of any human stock, or by the desire of a fleshly father, but . . . of God himself"[1].

Consider then this parable. John Doe, whom you know personally, is reported in the newspaper as having been arrested for embezzlement. Your reactions to this news will be either of the following. You may say, "I am not surprised: that is what I should have expected of him". Or you may say, "I cannot believe it; there must be some excuse for this that I do not know of." These reactions express your personal relation with John Doe. You *tend* either to believe ill of him, or to believe good. In the former case, detection of his dishonesty does not surprise you, and evidence of any faculty of self-denial in him would surprise you. In the second case, it would be the other way round. Your judgment of him, and your response to his actions, or his predicament, are settled by your prior attitude to him. Among sinners, there may be partial justification for your contempt; there may be no more than partial justification for your admiration. All that has happened before you were led to make that response to the crisis of John Doe has happened in the coarse texture of human life, and you may be

[1] St John 1:13.

entirely wrong in judging either way: you are not likely to be entirely right. But the very familiar fact that a response of this kind comes unpremeditated and usually goes before (and does not follow as the conclusion of) rational thought, makes it a reliable pointer to the tendencies of raw human nature. To some extent, if you said, "I am astonished that he should have done that", you not only show that you had faith in John Doe: you indicate that you do not propose entirely to renounce it. You will go to considerable lengths to persuade yourself, and perhaps others, that this, which has been publicly judged a crime, does not represent the real John Doe. On the other hand, if you said, "I am not surprised", you expressed the opposite of faith in John Doe (English has no word for faith's opposite). And you probably did so not because you knew John Doe to be an embezzler, not because he had borrowed five pounds from you and not returned it, but as likely as not because you saw, or thought you saw, in his habits of speech, his manner to his neighbours, a pattern of weakness and arrogance into which embezzlement, when it is proved, fits snugly.

Unfaith in God

John Doe and you are both sinners. But the Bible's diagnosis of the human predicament seems to be that men *tend* to speak of God as a man speaks of another man in whom he has no faith. The work of God in the world is evidenced by events; and the Scriptures divide humanity between those who say of a disaster, "That is not surprising: it is *just like* God to do that", and those who say, "I must be wrong if I ever think that the cruelty or heartlessness I see in this event is part of God's nature".

Events are accompanied by a moral law "in our members"[1] of which humanity tends either to say, "This privation of liberty is a *typical* gesture of an unfriendly God", or to say, "If I find this irksome, I am wrong in assuming that God intends it so".

[1] Romans 7:23.

Events and the operation of moral law (in the Old Testament sense) take place in the field of the physical universe. This physical universe itself it is open to man to regard as a general conspiracy against his safety and peace, or as the evidence, which man will profit by detecting and tracing, of a power that is also love: so that one says either, "That is typical of an unfriendly God", or, "This, if I will find it out, points me towards a wisdom that is also love".

In the natural man there is, according to Scripture, a tendency to say of all evil, "That is typical of an unfriendly God". This attitude is in the end explicitly described as the attitude of unfaith. The transference to the opposite attitude is effected by what human experience can only describe as a gift. Into this matter I have already ventured to pursue a discussion in an earlier book, written some years ago, but still adequately expressive of how these matters have presented themselves to my mind.[1]

I am now concerned with the specific matter of reconciliation, which is the outward aspect of this transference of human relation with God from one of grievance to one of reciprocal confidence. I believe that the whole Old Testament story is concerned with the need for this, and the New Testament story with the method of its achievement. But the first place to which we must go is surely the Book of Job.

Job Insists on Justice

We turn to *Job*, because this book—or religious play—is a study in suffering. Moreover, it is a study in man's relations with God viewed as a function of suffering. The innocence of the sufferer is presupposed, and it at once sets aside from the discussion any consideration of suffering as the just consequence of error.[2] The sufferer in the story is a person wholly in harmony with his circumstances; there is no point of discord at which, until the intervention of the divine with which the story begins, Job's relation with his circumstances, and therefore

[1] *The Gift of Conversion*, Lutterworth, 1957.   [2] Job 1:8–11.

with their author, God, is anything but harmonious. The question is: if such a person suffers, will he be *irreconcilably* separated from God? Will he decide irrevocably that God is against him?[1] It is no part of the story to explain the existence of suffering. It is concerned only with the effect suffering has on the relations between a good man and God.

Observe then its argument. In the first place, Eliphaz, the first of Job's interlocutors, represents to him his duty to "turn to God".

> Let your religion reassure you;
>   your blameless life, let that encourage you!
> Think now, what guiltless man has ever perished?
>   when have the just ever been swept away? . . .
> Were I in your place, I would turn to God,
>   and before God lay my case,
> Who does great things beyond our ken,
>   marvels beyond our reckoning.[2]

In other words: God cannot be wrong. Submit! And Job's reply contains these words:

> If I sin, what harm is that to thee,
>   O thou spy upon mankind?
> Why must thou always find me in thy way,
>   why vex thyself with me?[3]

Job, then, rejects the argument that there must somewhere be a cause for this in his life that he has overlooked. The author of the play has already stated that there is no such cause. "Religion" and a "turning to God" on the assumption of guilt is therefore no universal cure for suffering, and the explanation of suffering is not always to be found in error. (Sometimes it

[1] ib. 1:11.   [2] ib. 4:6–7; 5:8–9; translation of Dr Moffat.
[3] ib. 7:20.

may be: sometimes the moral approach *may* be right: but the play is asking, what is *always* right?).

Bildad, the second of his friends, takes up the same tale. God is just, and He is just as human beings understand justice. There is no future in attempting to refute God's argument that sorrow follows error.[1]

After Job answers Bildad with an outburst of passion which surrounds a strong plea to God to be rational, to state his case,[2] Zophar, his third friend, restates the case for divine justice in more offensive and trenchant terms, and with it the case for Job's making an act of contrition. And this brings from Job a long speech which contains one of the many passages in the book made familiar by quotation: "Though he slay me, yet will I trust in him." But the more accurate and also more vivid rendering which Dr Moffatt gives leaves us with something far from the impression of heroism that the familiar words convey:

He may kill me—what else can I expect?—
but I will maintain my innocence to his face.[3]

It may be necessary to interpolate here a defence of Dr Moffatt's audacious translation. Briefly, the notion in the verb "trust" is an illegitimate translation of the Hebrew and hardly better than a doubtful translation of the Vulgate *sperabo* ("I will hope"). It cannot mean more than "I wait". If this much weaker verb be allowed to replace the highly evocative "trust", and the "although" consequent on the use of "trust" be dropped altogether, we have: "He will kill me: I will wait: I will maintain my innocence." The effect then is not one of religious resignation, but on the contrary of defiance. Moffatt's "what else can I expect?" is an interpretation: but undoubtedly its tendency is in a direct line with the plot of the story.

Job's contention is, then, that whatever happens he will insist, unless God openly shows where he had done wrong, that he is innocent. Considered as the creature of his author,

[1] ib. ch. 8.   [2] ib. 10:2.   [3] ib. 13:15.

Job stands for the principle that suffering and error are not to be indissolubly linked.

A Vindicator

Now the argument of the play continues from that point through a perfectly predictable course. It is not necessary here to follow it closely for the rest of its length. We may pause only to take note of another mistranslated passage which has become extremely familiar, outside its context, through wide popular use. This is the verse where he says, "I know that my Redeemer liveth", and in which again he is represented by the familiar translation as speaking more religiously, more prophetically, than his author intended. The true meaning of this passage is pivotal to the whole argument of this present book, and (what is somewhat more important) to the doctrine of reconciliation to which the New Testament provides the key.

Badgered as he is by the continual appeals of his friends to a religious outlook which is too irrational for him, and which insists on missing the precise points of his condition: tantalized and vexed beyond measure at his friends' fumbling ineptitude in trying to treat his situation as though it were another and more familiar situation, Job enters on that immortal speech which is recounted in chapter 19.

> How long will you harrow my soul,
>   and crush me with your words?
> Time and again you have taunted me,
>   you have wronged me shamelessly.
> Supposing I have sinned,
>   does my sin injure you?
> Are you to lord it over me,
>   and to reproach me with my misery?
> Understand, it is God who has undone me,
>   and spread his nets around me.
> I cry out "Murder!": there is no reply;
>   I call for help, and get no justice. . . .

O that my defence were written,
    oh that my case could be preserved in writing,
cut with an iron pen on lead,
    or lastingly engraved on stone!

Still, I know One to champion me at last,
    to stand up for me upon earth.
This body may break up, but even then
    my life shall have a sight of God;
my heart is pining as I yearn
    to see him on my side,
    see him estranged no longer.[1]

The real question here is, of course, who is this, who is
represented by the word "Redeemer" in the AV, "Vindicator"
in other translations, and here by the phrase "One to champion
me"—the capital letter in the pronoun indicating, one must
suppose, an angelic or divine being? It is Christ only by
typology: and that typology turns out to involve a very
hazardous leap of thought.

There are certain evident difficulties in this utterance
which are probably easily resolved if we take care to elimin-
ate, at any rate at the outset, New Testament ideas from the
words written. It is not necessary, surely, in the first place,
to insist that Job is here enunciating a doctrine of Resurrection, or of future life (which doctrine is, of course, only
hinted at in the Old Testament, and normally then only
through words of protest against the futility of death, such
as those in Ps 30:9). His body may break up—death and
dissolution are the ultimate point of the sufferings he is
already undergoing. But at the heavenly Assize he believes
that he will have a defender. Is it obligatory to suppose that
he means that *after his death* he will "have a sight of" God?
It is surely preferable, and more in harmony with Old
Testament theology, to suppose his author to be causing
him here to say in effect, "the reconciliation will be effected,

[1] ib. 19:1–7, 23–7.

and I shall know it". For the traditional assumption that no man may see God and live (cf. Ex 33:20) is bound up with the idea that it is man's sin that makes him unable to bear this sight.

"There's Been a Mistake"

No, the Advocate whom he looks for is, in one special sense, not Jesus Christ. His statement of hope is indeed a great leap of faith: but it is faith in the justice of God, a justice which, as he has kept on saying, it is he, Job, who is defending, and his interlocutors who are traducing. Their makeshift and formal religion does violence to justice, which is (whatever else) reasonable: his insistence on his innocence is a way of saying, "God is just, and I mean to see this justice vindicated".

But in that case what Job is now saying is, "There has been some mistake!" He cannot bring himself to say that God is wrong; but he pictures God as a judge who misdirects his jury because important information has been withheld. Somebody, a "Vindicator", a "One to champion me at the last" will produce the information, correct the mistake, and cause God to pronounce an acquittal.

This "Somebody" is a product of hope. He is an impersonation of Job's unshakeable conviction in God's justice. He will be the agent of reconciliation, and after his intervention God will be "estranged no longer". No more than that can be read into Job's climactic cry; but it is not for that any less a gesture of faith at the highest Old Testament level.

But the "Somebody" is one who, in the divine Assize, will argue with God, will defend Job against God, and will bring God's views round to a position more favourable to Job.

What this exposes at once is that condition in the human predicament which it is the peculiar office of Christ, the Son of God, to correct. This is the assumption that God is not well-disposed to men, and that Somebody must win back His favour. The assumption that God does not love the world, and cannot do so until somebody has represented the world to Him in a favourable light, is an Old Covenant notion of atonement: if you will, it is a naturalistic view of atonement. But it is not what we read of in the Gospels. What Job's affirmation amounts to is the highest and noblest thing a man could say, given the assumption that God is, at present, holding the world in disfavour. There is no detraction from God's character. Mankind may deserve this disfavour. The sentence may in general be just. Either a man must accept the sentence, or he must show himself to be guiltless of his charge. How he is to be "justified" before God[1] is the peculiar problem of innocent suffering. If there is nothing a man can do to show his innocence, he must fall under the judgment and accept the sentence. But this would be to make God, in his case (in Job's case) unjust, and *ex hypothesi* this is impossible. Then he must believe that "Somebody" will set things right.

Now the end of the Job story is august, majestically set forth in incomparable language (whether in the original or in English): its end is a happy one in that, having seen the *power* of God, superbly deployed in all the colourful magnificence and terrifying variety of the created world, Job says, "Now I see". This makes a conclusion of incomparable literary beauty, but theologically entirely unsatisfying. It is simply not true that a good long look at the wonders revealed by astronomers, and a trip round the world to see the Himalayas and the beasts of the jungle and the wastes of the Arctic, will bring a man to reconciliation with God. There is no more universal truth in the author of *Job*'s solution than in the original hypothesis that suffering is a symptom of sin. This we can say because as Christians we know that the end of Job's story is not at the end of chapter 42, but in the Passion and Resurrection of Christ. This is, by the way, not a return to that typology which we have just stated to be hazardous; nor is it a capitulation to "Biblical theology". It is, if we say that the story of Job is an essay in the problem of reconciliation, precisely the truth. What Christ did for the world cannot be more exactly stated than by saying that He became exactly that

[1] ib. 25:4.

"Somebody" of whom Job spoke: but that in doing so he showed us that we had in one important particular been telling the wrong story altogether.

For Jesus Christ did not come to stand for us over against God: to vindicate mankind against a God who disbelieved in man's worthiness to be saved. It was precisely towards the eradicating of this persistent illusion—an illusion which continued through the days of His incarnation and has ever since been the chief source of the church's errors—that His teaching was directed.

CHAPTER II

The Reconciler

Is the Gospel-Record Evidence?

WE must first settle one preliminary question: in what sense we are here to take the Gospel records as carrying authority. The reader will not need to be reminded of the danger of basing arguments on the literal interpretation of short texts in the Gospels (or anywhere else) removed from their contexts; although it might be as well to remark that what we often mean by "taking literally" is the interpretation of English words according not only to an English sense which may not be the sense their writers meant them to carry, but also to a sense which is conditioned by all manner of thought-habits peculiar to our own age and far distant from the writer's imagination. "Though he slay me, yet will I trust in him" is a case in point. Not only is it not what its Hebrew author meant to make Job say: it is not now by any means exactly what its translator (even if here he was a mistranslator) meant us to understand. The curiously heroic and chivalrous ring that the words now have is full of associations which would not have occurred to that seventeenth-century translator. "Blessed are the meek" is an equally obvious example from the Gospels. "Meek" may well have been an excellent translation of the Greek word *praeis*: but its associations are nowadays very wide of the mark at which the author of the Gospel and his AV translator were aiming.

All this is familiar to any serious reader of Scripture. What we are now, however, bound to make up our minds about is the extent to which we can trust the Gospel record as a reliable record of the acts and words of an historical Jesus. We know that at many points adjustments must be made to the text if we are to come by anything like an accurate record of what was actually said or done—for example, in the incident concerning the fig-tree in Mark 11:12–14 and 20–1. There some believe that what is recorded as a "miracle" was in fact no more than a spoken parable.[1] When commentators and scholars have shown quite legitimate grounds for doubt whether we ought always to take the Gospel record as a directly historical record of things that here or there are said to have happened, doubt spreads, and in the end we are obliged to formulate a theory of authority which will not be disturbed by the occasional demonstration that the Gospel deviates from historic accuracy.

This has all manner of consequences which others have ably exposed. For our present purpose it is only necessary to say explicitly what ground we think we are standing on when we seek to extract evidences from the Gospel text. For my own part, I am prepared to say this: that if sufficient agreement on a point of broad principle is to be found in a large number of Gospel texts, if no contradiction of the point of principle can be found in any other texts, and especially if these texts come from parts of the Gospel whose form and style are of varying kind, then we can regard the principle as established.

I shall produce in a moment evidences for the point I am concerned with that come from many parts of all four Gospels, and that are taken from records not only of the sayings but also of the actions of Jesus. I am personally disposed to say that I believe that he said and did these things. But if a consensus of scholarly opinion ultimately persuades us all that not one of these sayings or actions is reported with historical accuracy, then I should still say that *The Gospel*, as it is recorded by these four witnesses, seems to be of a common mind on the matter. If I am required to refrain from saying that "Jesus", the historical Person, said or did any of these things, it is still of enormous importance to note that his four witnesses insist that He did say *this kind of thing*. Since I am not concerned with

---

[1] Actually, I still stand by my own conjecture on this passage in *The Gift of Conversion*, pp. 100–1.

any particular thing that He is said to have said or done, but with the total effect of almost everything that He is said to have said and done, it may well be that I am telling my reader only about the opinions of the four Evangelists, and that neither I nor anybody else can tell him what Jesus really did say and do. I hasten to say that personally I do not think that the four Evangelists, whoever they were, can possibly have been members of a conspiracy to attribute to Christ teachings opposed to what he taught: for if this is the case, what purpose is served by mentioning Christ at all? But if my evidences are taken by any to be evidences of what the Evangelists say, and not evidences of what the Lord said and did, they are still of great importance for Christian doctrine and practice; because it is the consensus of the vast majority of Christians that Scripture is the ground of all authority in the Church: and even if Scripture is not the absolutely clear historical record that it was perhaps once taken to be, none the less for that it is the only record the church has, and its content and limits are precisely the consequence of the church's primitive faith in their authenticity as conveying the Truth, even if they are now felt to convey it otherwise than historically at certain points.

Rather often I shall have to say, "Jesus said this", or, "Jesus did that", giving a Gospel reference. I am quite prepared to be taken as saying, "Mark says Jesus said this", or, "John says Jesus did that", and for my conclusions to suffer any limitation of relevance that follows from this admission. But to avoid cumbersome circumlocutions I shall not every time qualify such statements by putting them into reported speech. I do not feel that this concession makes the least difference to an argument which is concerned with the everyday faith of the Christian. Such a faith is based on a revelation, and the Gospels provide this revelation for us. What then do they say?

God Always Loved

They say—to state my conclusion at once—that there was a certain unique quality in the ministry of Jesus which made him the author of a dispensation which the greatest of the prophets[1] never entered. The area in which this uniqueness shows itself is the area of reconciliation between man and God. Given the condition of sin (and sin is a concept which before we are done we must bring to definition) the Old Dispensation could think, as Job thought, only of a mediator between God and man who would turn aside God's anger and invoke God's favour. Such were the priests of the Old Testament, and such in their way were the prophets. Atonement was really "propitiation" (and the celebrated mistranslation resulting in "propitiation" in the AV of I John 2:2 was a great disaster because it directly obscured this difference between the Old and the New views of reconciliation). The office of Jesus was not to represent men to God, but to *be* God among men. Where men were saying constantly just what Job had said: "God must be caused to love the world", Jesus said, He only could say, "God is love"— meaning "God loves the world and has always loved it". The familiar words in John 3:16 beginning "God loved the world so much" (NEB) must never be taken as meaning that in the sending of His Son, God began to love the world.

Therefore, if ever any person who encountered Jesus appeared to be falling into the error of saying, "God hates me, but you love me", Jesus gave an unambiguous indication that this is the opposite of the effect he intended his ministry to have.

Reconciliation, in the unique New Testament sense, is not the bringing together of two parties who have fallen out, offence on the one side provoking anger on the other, retaliation on the second part being resented on the first. It is the restoration of a relation between two parties which one party broke by assuming in the other party a hostility which was never there.

Sin

This is why the equating of "sin" with "errors" is so fertile a source of perverse religious teaching. Whatever is done in colloquial speech, or in legitimate shorthand or small-talk of reli-

[1] Matt 11:11.

gious intercourse, the distinction in kind between sin and error must always be preserved. Wrong action is always the consequence of sin: but it is not its only consequence. When John the Baptist referred to Christ as "The Lamb of God . . . who takes away the sin of the world"[1] he cannot possibly have meant that Jesus would remove from the world error, pain, deformity and wickedness. He did mean that He would remove what caused these things: that He was Himself the removal of these things.

From its first mention of the condition, the Old Testament promotes the doctrine that sin is a settled attitude towards God on man's part that can best be described by the English word "grievance".[2] The story of Eden introduces the error of Eve by presenting "Adam" not as an adventurous rebel "chancing his arm" against authority and proving his freedom and manhood in the act, but as one into whose mind the thought has been introduced that God's reason for making a certain prohibition was a self-regarding one: that God is "against" mankind *a priori*. Nothing else can be gathered from Gen 3:5 than that in the religious folklore of ancient Israel it was a sense of grievance rather than a sense of adventure that produced the first breach of confidence between man and God. The insistence of the more perceptive of the prophets on God's utter innocence of any tyrannous or oppressive intention towards mankind makes the same point. Jeremiah is the most conspicuous example, especially in the thought of his early chapters: but Hosea in making a parable out of his own life takes exactly the same line. True, much of the OT's religious interpretation of history proceeds on the assumption that men will be punished by God for their misdeeds, and that only by open confession of their errors will they turn aside the punishment that otherwise is justly ordered. But this is secondary. It is a natural outcome of man's prior conviction that God is, *a priori* and for

1 John 1:29.
2 I made this point in a simple way in *Beginning the Old Testament* (SCM, 1962) pp. 28–9.

no reason that man could have avoided by rectitude, against him.

This is the general drift of the argument which the Gospels seem to support. It presupposes that sin is not comprehended in any wrong action, however obviously and universally hideous that action is. Ultimate sin is not even in blaspheming against the name of Jesus.[1] Sin is essentially a settled condition of grievance against God, entered into by an act of decision. It is nothing else. Wrong action springs from nothing else, for an action is in the ultimate sense wrong only because it does have this origin. It is not "in order to make us good" that Christ died, but in order to make us enjoy the goodness of God.

Sin and Deformity

We may first consider the incidents in the Gospels in which Jesus is recorded as having done works of healing, and as having indicated in his words a connection between deformity and "unreconciled-ness", i.e., sin. At the healing of the paralytic in Mark 2:1–12, "When Jesus saw their faith, he said to the paralysed man, 'My son, your sins are forgiven'." This aroused the indignation of the orthodox who heard him; but he insisted that this was the right response to the man's need. There is essentially no difference between say "stand up and walk" and "your sins are forgiven", if what is in view is a real healing.

No more is said at that point, and the onlookers are understandably left wondering. But in another incident of healing a paralytic, in John 5:1–15, the healing of the malady and the reference to sin appear to be separated by an interval of time. Here it seems that the sufferer is healed, and after he has enjoyed the effect of the healing for a while Jesus meets him—"a little later" is the phrase in the text.[2] At this second meeting he says, "Now that you are well again, leave your sinful ways, or you may suffer something worse". What can be meant here but that the enjoyment of good health is in itself no more than a physical restoration of harmony; in itself it does not lead

---

[1] Matt 12:32.   [2] John 5:14: further comment below, p. 47.

automatically to a restoration of the sufferer's relation with God.

On the contrary—and this is where we touch the nerve of the argument—what might easily happen is that the sufferer, who is described in the evangelist's account as a person much given to grievance against his circumstances, might go among his friends and say, "God afflicted me, and this man Jesus has cured me. I always said that God is against me, but I was lucky to find this man who is on my side". This would indeed, from the point of view of the atoning ministry of Jesus, be a total disaster. It is a monstrous inversion of the purpose of Christ when the benefits he confers become in themselves a new excuse for believing in God's hostility. But the extent to which ordinary experience shows how easily this can come about will be a matter for consideration later.

As Mark's Gospel proceeds we encounter another episode, to which we have already made passing reference, which states the same truth in a different mode. Our Lord's very stern words about the sin of "slander against the Holy Spirit"[1] are provoked by the Pharisaic comment that his "casting out of devils"—which refers to healing of physical or mental illness—is the result of a treaty between Jesus and the prince of the devils: in other words, that it is witchcraft. This is so exactly the opposite of the truth that it is the only context in which Jesus can intelligibly speak of the ultimate sin. His purpose in all his healings is to bring man towards God, to eradicate his hostility to God and his assumption of God's hostility. The insistent and ultimate perseverance in that assumption, in the face of all evidences rational and supernatural, is naturally the ultimate sin: there is no forgiveness for it because it renders the sinner incapable of receiving forgiveness: he, the sinner, cannot believe there is any such thing as forgiveness from God to himself: if forgiveness were spoken it would be in a language unintelligible to him, or at a sound-level outside the range of his ears. This could only be said when the critics of Jesus had

[1] Mark 3:22–30. In Matt 12:22–32 the nature of the sin and the context of the utterance are made more explicit.

provided a context by saying that his ministry is a treaty with the devil—the diametric opposite of a reconciliation with God.

There is another healing-miracle, recorded only by St Luke, which brings out the same point even more forcibly. On a certain occasion, ten lepers are healed of their disorder.[1] Of these "one, finding himself cured, turned back, praising God aloud". Jesus says, "Were not all ten cleansed?... Could none be found to come back and give praise to God, except this foreigner?" And he said to the man, "Stand up, and go on your way; your faith has cured you."

It would be artificial to insist on what seems to be the different force of "cleanse" and "cure" in that passage; although the Greek behind "cleanse" means indeed literally "cleanse", while the Greek behind the NEB's "cure" is the word usually translated "saved". The AV here has, as in Mark 6:34, "hath made thee whole": for "saved" means "rescued", and no doubt in such a place as this means "delivered from the bondage of disease"—but also "of sin".

"Give Glory to God"

The central point is quite clear. This Samaritan leper was going about *giving glory to God.* It is not his returning to thank *Jesus* that matters so much, although it is because he did so that Jesus was able to draw attention to what did matter. Jesus did not praise the leper for having the grace to say "Thank you" to himself. He commended him for praising God—the God in whom he, the Samaritan leper, had always believed, but to whom he had now been enabled to turn as a son turns to his father. And this, you will observe (having regard to what we said earlier in the context of *Job*) Jesus calls *faith.* What the other nine lepers were doing we do not know. Jesus did not claim that he knew. They may have been praising God, although they did not return to Jesus and do it in his presence. It is not, of course, the way of Jesus to denounce those who miss the great blessings, but rather to draw attention to those who attain

[1] Luke 17:11–19.

them. This, the cleansing of leprosy plus the praising of God, is the real cure. The others are technically cleansed. This man is free ("saved").

"Saving Faith"

Faith (*pistis*) is, then, often associated with this restoration of the relation of trust between man and God. It must be one of the many facets of the meaning of this strange word, that it implies the decision that reverses the old decision—the first decision which we included in our definition of sin (a settled state of grievance entered into by an act of decision).

True, as the text stands, it is not normally possible to justify fully this interpretation of "faith" in the cures of Christ from the words and context. In Mark we have three instances: the faith of the stretcher-bearers (2:5), the faith of the woman in the crowd (5:34), and the faith of the blind man (10:52), in the two last of which the expression "Your faith has cured you" is used. Matthew adds the faith of the centurion (8:10), the faith of the two blind men (9:29), if that story be not a doublet of the Bartimaeus legend, and the faith of the Canaanite woman (15:28). Luke adds only the incident of the lepers which we have just mentioned.

In all these cases "faith" seems to mean the same thing, and it does not at first appear to be what we have suggested it means in Luke 17:19. It appears to be a pertinacious belief in the personal power of Christ to heal. The overcoming of difficulties is always implied. The stretcher-bearers found a novel way of getting to Jesus when no other presented itself; the woman with the haemorrhage battled her way through the crowd; the blind men insisted (see e.g. Mk 10:48) against the repressive suggestions of the bystanders, on being heard; the centurion went far out of his way in personally going to Jesus instead of sending a messenger; the Canaanite woman showed wit and courage in her spirited reply to the strange testing words of Jesus. Nothing in the text suggests that Jesus uses the word "faith" to mean the inception of a new relation between the sufferer and God. He seems only to be describing the sufferer's (or his friends') attitude to himself.

That must for the present be admitted. If we want to find in "faith" in these contexts more than an attitude towards the healing power of Jesus, we shall have to use other evidences to establish it.

"Tell Nobody"

But other evidences there certainly are. Returning to one of the points made above in connection with the story in John 5:1–15, we will consider the very clear evidences given to us of the attitude of Jesus towards his own healing ministry. In the first place, there are the many occasions when he gave a strict instruction that the matter should not be broadcast.

There is the leper in Mark 1:43, who is told to do what is technically necessary to obtain a certificate of clearance, but to tell nobody but his doctor of what has happened. To the blind men whose healing is recorded in Matt 9:27–31 "Jesus said . . . sternly, 'See that no one hears about this'." The dumb man healed at Decapolis (7:36) is similarly told to be silent. In none of these cases was the injunction obeyed; in the first of them Jesus had to leave the district and hide himself. In the last, "their astonishment knew no bounds: 'All that he does, he does well', they said, 'he even makes the deaf hear and the dumb speak'."[1] But glowing though the testimonies were, Jesus did not wish for them. And his rejection of the fame and praise that such reports would bring him must be all of a piece with his rejection, on the one hand, of any attempt to give him public honour (as in John 6:15, with which compare the whole trend of the second and third of his Temptations) and his insistence, on the other, on speaking "only in parables" (Mark 4:34). What was the danger to His ministry inherent in the broadcasting of His fame as a worker of healing miracles, in the accepting of public honour, in the assumption of the role of popular preacher? The immediate consequence, one would

[1] Mark 7:37.

think, would be the wider efficacy of His ministry; but to say that is to assume that the purpose of His ministry was to *be* immediately effective, to touch as many people as possible, and to establish Himself as a public benefactor. Place it as high as you will: say (as people often do say of the Christian ministry) that the right course is to take every possible opportunity of making known the vital truth of God's love to the world, and that no fear of being thought a vulgar publicist should deter such a messenger of grace from taking these steps: you will still be as far as ever from that understanding of His ministry which Jesus, on the Gospel evidences, intended to convey.

The danger was precisely that people should "make Him a king". And they have no king but God. "Good Master", said the eager young man, "What shall I do—?" "Why do you call me good? None is good, except God alone."[1] Either we must say that *that* is the note constantly struck in the work and words of Christ, or we must explain his hatred of publicity as a mere expedient. And the highest value we can put, in human terms, on His rejection of public acclaim is trivial compared with what must be the real explanation: that men would, given the least chance, divert to Him the praise that was due to God. That they would love Him and continue to hate God.

An Exception?

Now there is one place in the earlier part of the Gospel story where Jesus seems to have taken a different line. This is in that spectacular incident in which, at the expense of a herd of pigs, a lunatic was healed in the Gergesene country. Whether the Master gave his permission to broadcast the cure partly because already the incident had attracted such unusual attention, or whether his permission had to do with the different ethos of the locality in which the incident took place are matters of conjecture secondary to what emerges from the text as it lies before us at Mark 5:19. Explicitly refusing to allow the man to become a disciple in the "inner circle", Jesus says to the

[1] Luke 18:19.

healed lunatic: "Go home to your own folk, and tell them what the Lord in his mercy has done for you." "The Lord" here is God the Father. Luke says so explicitly.[1] Why this form of positive command is substituted here for the earlier prohibition we cannot know: but the form of the positive command is clear enough. "Go and tell of what God in his mercy has done for you." There was probably little chance, in a place from which Jesus had been asked to depart at once (Matt 8:34) that the publicity would draw undesirable attention to the person of Jesus. But the opportunity for witnessing to the love of God was at once to be grasped.

"Publicity" or "Glory"

This is a formal rather than an essential exception. The aim of Jesus is to make it as difficult as he can for men to divert to Himself the praise due to God. But (we shall discuss this in a moment) John's witness to his ministry does show that in a certain sense he *did* wish to attract the attention of the community amongst which he moved.

We shall see that in the sense of "manifesting his glory" (John 2:11, for example) Jesus was prepared to use the power of publicity. But we shall also see that this "glory" was precisely intended to be an extinction of Himself and a showing forth of the Father. In the last weeks of His ministry, Jesus seems to have been no longer interested in keeping Himself hidden from the multitude's adoration. But this was when it was clear not only to Himself but to all who were close to Him that this publicity would lead directly not to a throne but to a cross. The beginning of the change (though not, in the Gospel record, the end of the prohibitions on advertisement) is signified by the synoptic evangelists as being at Caesarea Philippi: possibly St John's counterpart to this is at 6:69: and if the conjecture that his sixth chapter should precede his fifth is right, it makes it much easier to see in that Gospel how the transition was made from a "private" to a "public" ministry. But of course this

[1] Luke 8:38.

does involve us in accepting that John puts the change in our Lord's attitude (foreshadowed in "My hour has not yet come", John 2:4) chronologically earlier than the Synoptics put it. This is in no way an obstacle to the progress of our present argument.

CHAPTER III

The Messiah

A Messianic Consciousness?

IT is at this point that we must introduce the matter of the Messiahship of Jesus into this discussion. There has been much discussion and speculation on the question, to what extent and in what mode Jesus was Himself conscious of His Messiahship: and while such debate is legitimate, and at many points illuminating, in the nature of things it is concerned with a question which can find no certain answer.

Professor John Knox has a statement of a conservative and, as I believe, wholly reasonable opinion on this august subject in his book, *The Death of Christ*. There he writes:

The life of Jesus is the most significant life ever lived, but no more in his case than in that of any lesser figure of history does the truth of our estimate depend upon our finding that he himself placed the same value upon the significance of his career. The Christian faith is not a belief that Jesus entertained certain ideas, which therefore must be true; it is rather the conviction, grounded in the concrete realities of the Church's life (including the memory of Jesus himself) that his career was the central element in a divine and supremely significant event. That Jesus himself was sensitive to the uniqueness and urgency of the crisis in the midst of which he stood and to its divine meaning, we can be indubitably sure. And assurance on this point enables us to find a closer coherence and a deeper unity in the event than would otherwise appear. Indeed, it is hard to see how, without such awareness on his part, the event could have come to pass at all. But we do not need to go further and ascribe to him definite ideas about his own nature or office. Such ascriptions not only often fail to assist or support our faith in Christ, they may even burden and obstruct it.[1]

In the course of the argument which leads up to this conclusion, Prof. Knox disposes of the notion that Jesus was especially conscious of himself as fulfilling the role of Isaiah's "Suffering Servant", and he also argues that the idea of the "Son of Man" as it stood in OT apocalyptic was not one which he primarily wished to have applied to himself.[2]

A Danger in Typology

The application of these Old Testament notions to Christ can, as Prof. Knox implies, be tainted with the weakness that all typologies suffer from. It is possible to detract from the uniqueness of Jesus by pressing too firmly and literally the idea that in him "the Scriptures are fulfilled". To be sure, all his actions and sayings are very deeply rooted in Scripture; it is this—to say no more of it—that made them intelligible to any of his contemporaries who did understand them. That the Scriptures —and especially the literature of the Psalms—provide the thought-forms of so much of his speech, and the act-forms of so many of his significant actions (one needs only to think of the relation between the teaching associated with the Feeding of the Five Thousand and the Exodus in John 6, or between the events of the first day of the Passion week and other OT prophecies) is beyond doubt: but the author of *Matthew*, in his zeal for finding and identifying Old Testament parallels for the great moments of the Gospel, must not divert us from taking a duly reverent and modest view of our capacity to analyse the Master's psychology. Scripture is not only a record of Israel's history: it is part of that history: and our Lord's use of it in his words and acts is better thought of as illustrative than as designed to add any authority to those words and acts. He will use Scripture equally to illustrate, or to provide

[1] J. Knox, *The Death of Christ* (Collins, 1959), pp. 124–5.
[2] Knox, *op. cit.*, chapter IV.

a familiar context for, His teaching (as in John 6:30–40) and to provide ground for refuting the attacks of his enemies (as in John 5:45–7 and 8:31–58); but we cannot possibly regard Him as in any sense conditioned at the centre of His mind by Scripture: He is its fulfilment, but not its creature.

Messiahship Is Self-Destruction

The one thing that is perfectly clear about His Messianic consciousness is that He regarded His Messiahship as centred on an act of self-destruction. As the Synoptic Gospels report Him—and in this the first three are in agreement not only verbally but in the order in which they place the events—Jesus chose a certain moment, at Caesarea Philippi, to reveal the nature of His Messiahship to his friends. The question was asked of Peter, and out of Peter's mouth came the critical words: "You are the Messiah".[1] At once a description of his Messiahship follows. This draws from Peter a protest which represents the whole of our human predicament when Messiahship confronts us. The Scriptural Messiah (who is, of course, largely a creature of apocalyptic) is not a Suffering Servant but a conqueror, a liberator, a *Son of God* who looks and acts as human beings expect a Son of God to look and act. No matter how much the disciples had heard from Jesus of the necessity for self-denial, of the self-destructive pattern of the Christian life (and it must be observed that it is after, not before Caesarea Philippi, that this kind of teaching is, according to the Synoptics, made explicit), Messiahship is to them the office of the conqueror, not of the crucified. Peter's protest is just what a Messiah-conscious Israelite must make. And it must at once be clearly rejected by Jesus as Satan's doctrine. This, precisely, is what he has come to correct: this is what he has come to judge.

Now it may be observed that at Caesarea Philippi Jesus repeats the injunction that he had given to those whom earlier he had healed: "he gave them strict orders not to tell anyone

[1] Mark 8:29. Matt 16:16. Luke 9:21.

about him."[1] After the Transfiguration, which forms a climax to the teaching on the implications of this Messiahship on his disciples, he says the same.[2] Of the teaching that came between the revelation at Caesarea Philippi and the Transfiguration, which enjoined on all His followers the duty of self-denial and self-destruction, Mark and Luke significantly say that it was given not only to the disciples, but to "the people" (Mark)— "all present" (Luke)—as well.[3] The teaching about self-denial is for all: the specific revelation that He is Messiah is still only for the few, and it does not look as if they are going to understand it.

All popular notions of "The Messiah" are repudiated

The revelation of Himself to "all" becomes gradual. He is now, anyhow, prepared to speak about "The Messiah" in general terms, and to take what opportunities are offered to correct the popular notions of what should be expected of the Messiah. In the Temple-debates of the last Week, for example, He finds occasion to say:

How can the teachers of the law maintain that the Messiah is "Son of David"? David himself said, when inspired by the Holy Spirit, "The Lord said to my Lord, 'Sit at my right hand until I make your enemies your footstool'." David himself calls him "Lord"; how can he also be David's son?[4]

The Messiah is not Messiah because he is "son of David". There is no derivation from David, physical or historical, that confers Messiahship in this new sense.

Jesus is not publicly claiming to be Messiah yet. He is only saying what people must expect the Messiah to be. And quoting "David" (meaning the Psalmist, and subsuming under "David" all Old Testament religious thought) he says that the Messiah is somebody whom David will be calling "Lord". David will be abased before this wonder, this portent, as much as anybody

[1] Mark 8:30, Matt and Luke agree.
[2] Mark 9:9, Matt and Luke agree.
[3] Mark 8:34. Luke 9:23.   [4] Mark 12:35–7.

else: as much as Elijah and Moses were at the Transfiguration. David, Elijah and Moses will find their fulfilment here: but it will not be because This is a derivation from them and what they stood for. This is going to correct them, to destroy them, and in that judgment to bring them to the Resurrection. Jesus himself will not go straight to God's right hand and trample on his enemies, as "David's" Messiah does in Psalm 110. To human eyes he will be not glorified but destroyed: glorified only to the eye of faith.

This is the manner in which Jesus prepares His hearers for what they are so shortly to witness. He does it often, of course, by translating the principle of Messiahship into terms of discipleship. Just as the Messiah achieves his victory only through utter self-abasement, so his followers will achieve it by no other means. They cannot work a miracle of healing[1] just by announcing that they are his followers. They must be, as His words about prayer imply, reconciled men, men of the Messiah, not merely followers of Jesus of Nazareth. On the other hand, "if anyone gives you a cup of water to drink because you are followers of the Messiah, that man will assuredly not go unrewarded".[2] What is impossible for men, however devoted they may be to Jesus, like the young man who ran up and kneeling before him asked . . . "What must I do to win eternal life?"[3] is possible with God, and for God-filled and God-reconciled men. It is Messiahship that works the reconciliation through self-destruction, and that confers upon followers of the Messiah the power to live and act as men who are in the Kingdom. It is for this reason that Jesus keeps His first and last positive statement about His Messiahship for the moment when, humanly speaking, all is clearly lost. It is the High Priest Caiaphas who is privileged to hear Him answer the question, "Are you the Messiah?" with the words, "I am".[4]

On two other occasions, both of which are private and the first of which records a repetition of the injunction to secrecy,

---

[1] Mark 9:23.   [2] Mark 9:41.   [3] Mark 10:25.
[4] Mark 14:61, Matt 26:63 and Luke 22:70 put it somewhat differently, but we may well believe that Mark's simple report is the correct one.

Jesus speaks of the pattern of His Atonement in terms of self-destruction and resurrection.[1] In both these cases, as at Caesarea Philippi, and as recorded in all three Synoptic Gospels, our Lord uses the words "Son of Man". For the moment we shall accept the fact that this is the title He almost always prefers to "Messiah": its special implications must be discussed in a moment. But on all these three occasions when He speaks of His approaching death and resurrection there are indications that the announcement troubled the disciples, or puzzled them.[2]

Now is what we are here saying a denial of the implication that Jesus always seems to have associated a prediction of Resurrection with that of His death? This raises another important and pressing problem: that of the relation of the Resurrection to what we are insisting on as the self-destructive centre of the Messiahship of Jesus.

But Messiahship Is Still Liberation

The point which must not be lost sight of is that "Messiah" was a notion constantly present to the minds of the community out of which the disciples were drawn, but was a notion which Jesus was more concerned to correct than to confirm. The only point in common between what He wanted them to understand and what they already understood by the "Messiah" seems to be that of *liberation*. From that point on, the two ideas diverge. It is not liberation from a political oppression that Jesus seeks, but liberation from the moral, metaphysical bondage of "sin". And whereas liberation from political oppression may obviously be achieved by an open and evident victorious *coup* on the part of a revolutionary leader, the other liberation demands self-destruction, not self-exaltation. The ultimate outcome is a matter of the spirit, not of politics.

[1] Mark 9:30-2, 10:32-4: paralleled in Matt and Luke.

[2] In Luke 9:44-5, which corresponds with Mark 9:30-2, the speech of Jesus is much shorter, and the disciples' reaction is of incomprehension rather than grief. There is here no reference to the Resurrection. The deviation from the pattern set in the other passages is not important.

Therefore the disciples' notion of Messiahship is outraged.
The pattern of victory-through-self-destruction is to them a
frightening contradiction of what they had assumed. It is, indeed, a catastrophic correction of what during their association
with Jesus they had felt able to hope for. The astonishing
success of Jesus in His early ministry, His dramatic evidences
of divine power, were very much in line with that victorious
Messianic progress to which their people's teaching had led
them to look forward. They have now to reconstruct their ideas
not only of "the Messiah", but of what their own knowledge
of Jesus was supposed to lead to. These miracles, this teaching
of crowds, this authority and persuasive speech—all these are
not part of the build-up towards an earthly kingdom. They
are a build-up towards the kingdom that is "not of this
world".

It is perfectly plain that the "resurrection" prediction makes
no impact whatever on the disciples. What is less easy to be
sure of is whether the "Passion" prediction made any greater
impression.[1] But here I am concerned only with the question
whether the resurrection-prediction contradicts the assumption
that Messiahship showed itself to Jesus primarily in terms of
self-giving and self-destruction. It does not seem necessary to
admit that, because the whole prediction is a contradiction of
popular Messianic doctrine. It is so cast as to make the contradiction as stark as possible. It is not necessary to contradict the
popular assumption that the Messiah will conquer: but it is
necessary to contradict what the disciples think is to be the
pattern of that conquest. There is to be, not a straight run to
the throne, but death followed by that which alone can turn
death into part of a victory: resurrection.

[1] "There is every evidence that the disciples received and accepted the
forecast of death and acted precisely as might be expected in view of it.
There is no evidence that they received and accepted a forecast of resurrection, and every evidence that they did not act then or later in accordance
with such an expectation". Thus James McLeman in *The Birth of the
Christian Faith* (Oliver & Boyd, 1962). To the second proposition one is
obliged to assent: of the first there is surely some doubt. Mr McLeman
is contending that the forecasts of resurrection are suspect in any case.

Resurrection

Without doubt it is difficult to imagine what "resurrection" meant to anybody who had no knowledge of Christ's Resurrection and the Christian beliefs which are associated with it. What, for example, did "the resurrection" mean to those who wished to refute the Sadducees, who explicitly held "that there is no resurrection"?[1] This is a subject too large to enter on here: but Old Testament scholarship exposes many strands in Israel's speculation concerning a life after death. One of these is the moral sense which insists that in some condition which is not this life, the imperfections of this life will be healed and its injustices redressed, most impressively witnessed in Dan. 12:2: "Many of those who sleep in the dust of the earth shall awake, some to everlasting life, and some to shame and contempt:" this sense comes through in the Dives-Lazarus story which in Luke 16:19-31 Jesus adapts to his own purposes. On the other hand, there is a naturalistic protest against the idea that death must put an end to all those intimations of eternity which this life holds for mankind, which is witnessed in a place we have already mentioned, Psalm 30:5. Again, a resurrection-formula is employed by prophets who seek to offer hope to those to whom they speak, as does Hosea in Hos 6:1-2. Its association with God's judgment (a blending of the first and third senses) is found in the passage from which Paul quotes his famous "Death where is thy sting?" passage, Hos 13:14; and its association with a coming "golden age" is seen in Isaiah 24-27.[2] That there was an urge towards belief in a life beyond the present life is plain from many OT passages; such an urge to belief must lie behind the comment in Mark that suggests an eccentricity in the Sadducees' denial of it.

Now when Jesus refers to his Resurrection in such passages

[1] Mark 12:18.
[2] See H. H. Rowley, *The Faith of Israel* (SCM 1956) pp. 163-170 for comment on the association between expressions of Resurrection doctrine and the language of religions alien to that of Israel.

as those we are here discussing (with which no doubt the "Jonah" passage at Matt 12:39–40 must be associated), he is speaking, as he always spoke, in terms agreeable to the existing understanding of his hearers. If they are not to understand the Messiah as a conqueror in terms of this world, perhaps they will better appreciate the Messiah's true business if they understand his work in terms of another world—the world after which in their own way they have been groping. It is too soon yet to talk to them of the real content of the Resurrection as Christians will understand it. It is much more to the point to talk somewhat formally, and in a manner reminiscent of ancient prophecies such as Hosea's, of a resurrection "after three days", meaning no more, at this point, than an assurance that the Messiahship is to involve an act of self-destruction, but is not to be because of that a failure.

Resurrection-Predictions Do Not Contradict This View of Messiahship

I do not hold, with some sceptical scholars, that the predictions of the Resurrection attributed to Jesus are wholly to be suspected of spuriousness.[1] But I do believe that they are predictions only in a limited and general sense: only in a sense that would meet the understanding of those who heard them. Their limitation is not, however, so absolute as to make it necessary to alter anything they imply in the light of what did, according to the Gospels, happen. The transference of the Messianic office to a new plane is of the essence of the corrective teaching of Jesus. The spiritual and fundamental liberation effected by Jesus as Messiah will be as much a "new dimension" as is that which the OT writers indicated by their references to Resurrection: an age of redressed justice and

---

[1] McLeman, *op. cit.*, holds that they are spurious, and that the Caesarea-Philippi scene is a post-Resurrection story transferred by the primitive church to its present place.

healed woe, an age of revival, an age of transformation. What we do not hear in the Old Testament is what the New Testament explicitly gives us: that resurrection follows a *voluntary* self-destruction. The OT is concerned with getting somehow through the absurdity and outrage of death: death itself is unavoidable and imposed by God. Beyond it there may be something positive. The figure of death and resurrection, gathered originally of course from nature itself, is a convenient one to use for messages of hope. But to say, as Jesus is elsewhere recorded as saying, "The Father loves me because I lay down my life, to receive it back again. No one has robbed me of it; I am laying it down of my own free will",[1] and then to go on to apply this to the pattern of life, and death, required of the disciple, is something quite new. It is more even than is said in Isaiah 53, where there is no emphasis at all on the *voluntary* self-giving of the Servant, but only on the victory which comes to him through his *acceptance* of grief and slaughter.

It is Paul who constantly tells us in what dimensions, and with what rich adventures, we may think of the Resurrection. It is Paul who "demythologizes" the three-decker universe, and translates the old thought-form of "earth: under the earth: above the earth" into spiritual verities which apply throughout human life. It is he who tells us what it means to be "risen with Christ". What needs to be remembered here is only that when Jesus predicted His resurrection, He limited Himself to expressions that His followers could apprehend. To say more, (we do not know whether he would in any circumstances have done so) would be to travel too fast, and to blunt the edge of his specific contradiction of their error about Messiahship. What more has to be taught to His people he leaves, quite specifically, to the Holy Spirit's work, and it is as a promise of this that the last discourses of John are written. The contradiction itself is of the idea of a self-exalting Messiah: and the statement of Jesus about the Messiah, when He refers to

[1] John 10:18.

the idea at all, is a statement concerning the Messiah's self-giving.[1]

But this all becomes much clearer after we have entered deeper waters altogether, and considered what is the meaning, in Christ's teaching, of "sonship".

[1] See G. Bornkamm, *Jesus of Nazareth* (E.T. Hodder, 1960): "What astonishes us most is that Jesus does not directly make this claim [sc. of Messiahship] but lets it be absorbed in his words and works *without* justifying either in virtue of some office well known to his hearers, and *without* confirming the authority which the people are willing to acknowledge in him." (p. 170).

But note the comment on this passage in H. E. W. Turner, *Historicity and the Gospels* (Mowbray, 1963): "For Bornkamm the main titles which the Gospels describe as used by Jesus of himself must be regarded as the Credo of the believers and the teaching of the early Church rather than as authentic historical traditions . . . [For example] our Lord never claimed to be the Messiah. This may indeed be the historical kernel behind the theology of the Messianic Secret. But equally *to regard the ministry of Jesus as non-Messianic would be an over-simplification.*"

(My italics in both quotations).

CHAPTER IV

Father and Son

Self-Destruction Is "Glory"

SEVERAL times in the foregoing chapters I have used the word "self-destruction". I trust that none of my readers thinks that I mean by this "suicide". I mean, as the drift of my opening chapter implied, "destruction of *self*". We are now to turn to the evidences in the Fourth Gospel which support the view that throughout his ministry Jesus was systematically urging the principle of self-destruction as the principle of his ministry.

Nothing in the Fourth Gospel contradicts the evidences in the other three: but as might be expected the Fourth Evangelist approaches the whole matter from a new angle. The weight of his testimony concerning the person of Christ lies, of course, in the long discourses and debates which he records in chapters 5 to 17. The *actions* of Christ which he records are grouped (no doubt, selected) to form an ascending testimony to Christ's *glory*, in the sense that through them a certain kind of truth and grace was made manifest before the world: the discourses show in what sense this *glory* is in fact a subordination to the Father. It is not quite that it is merely a reflection of the Father: it is glory in that Jesus has submitted, of his own will, to the Father, and acknowledges and rejoices in his sonship. The discourses are therefore packed with references to "My Father". Let us amplify this.

John's Witness

John's approach to the "miracles" which he records is indicated in his use, in connection with them, of the words "sign" and "glory" (*semaion, doxa*). The words are used explicitly in four of the seven passages:

(1) This deed at Cana-in-Galilee is the first of the signs by which Jesus revealed his glory and led his disciples to believe in him. (2:11.)

(2) Will none of you ever believe without seeing signs and portents? (4:48.)

(3) I know that you have come looking for me because your hunger was satisfied with the loaves you ate, not because you saw signs. (6:26.)

(4) This sickness will not end in death; it has come for the glory of God, to bring glory to the Son of God. (11:4.)

These are the first, second, fourth and seventh of the miraculous actions of Christ recorded in John: the others are the healing of the paralytic (5:1–14), the walking on the water (6:16–21) and the giving of sight to the blind man (9:1–41). In the passages mentioned above "glory" appears in (1) and (4) and "sign" in (2) and (3). Whether it is positively the evangelist's intention that the words appear each time carrying a different sense in their context it would be too much to judge; but in (1), where we have both "sign" and "glory", the purpose of all the "miracles" is stated unambiguously. They were "signs" to communicate the "glory" of Jesus. A "sign" is what contains the truth concerning Jesus and his Father, and it is possible to see a "miracle" without seeing a "sign" (3); on the other hand a craving for a "sign", a thinking of a "sign" as a "proof" provided by God of His faithfulness before a man will have faith, is a wrong use of the "sign" (2) (cf. Matt 12:39). None the less, a situation which evokes the "miraculous" power of Jesus is one in which "glory" may be brought to God, and to the Son of God (i.e., in which "glory" may be clearly seen to be their possession) (4).

John's approach to the purpose of the "signs" is quite evidently different from that of the Synoptics; but as we hinted above (p. 22) he is primarily concerned to see the ministry of Jesus as a "manifestation of glory": and that glory is given to the Son by the Father. John therefore sees this as the central dynamic of the purpose of Jesus, and has less to say about the difference between His approach to His public ministry before and after the revelation of His Messiahship. It is only in 6:69 that he records anything like a critical decision on Peter's part, and there the context is of the desertion of Jesus by the crowds of admirers, not of Jesus Himself "coming out into the open".

But the views are, of course, not irreconcilable. They are different ways of presenting the subordination of Jesus Himself to the Father. If John, by placing the cleansing of the Temple so early, seems to be unconcerned to present the ministry as clearly divided between the period when Jesus wanted to show Himself in one way, and when He wanted to show Himself in another way, John none the less wants his readers to grasp the central purpose of Jesus in showing "such glory as befits the Father's only son".[1] With superb dramatic sense he then surprises his reader by showing him that this "glory" is in fact the cross itself: a "glory" in self-giving, received from the Father whose self-giving to the world the whole ministry of Jesus is designed to proclaim.[2]

The status of the seven "miracle" stories cannot entirely be tidied up, because the story in 6:16–21 about the walking on the water cannot without straining the text be incorporated into the pattern at all: and after all John had other purposes besides writing a source book for Christology. But the two other "miracle stories" we have referred to, which do not have an explicit mention of the words "sign" or "glory" happen to be stories of cures worked on the Sabbath. And this has, as John intends it to have, very important implications indeed.

The Sabbath—a Symbol of Reconciliation, Not Separation

The story in 5:1–15, we must now confess, has implications far beyond those which we mentioned in chapter 2. There we treated it as parallel to a "synoptic" miracle-story, and there was nothing wrong about so treating it. But its place in John

[1] John 1:14.   [2] John 17:22.

is determined by the fact that it leads straight into the first of the controversial discourses of Jesus, and the link between the action and the discourse is that of the Sabbath. The debate is introduced by the following words:

It was works of this kind done on the Sabbath that stirred the Jews to persecute Jesus. He defended himself by saying, "My Father has never yet ceased his work, and I am working too". This made the Jews still more determined to kill him, because he was not only breaking the Sabbath, but, by calling God his Father, he claimed equality with God.[1]

The ensuing debate is, of course, far more extended than anything which follows a "Sabbath" encounter in the Synoptics. Jesus defends His action at once in the words:

In truth, in very truth I tell you, the Son can do nothing of himself; he does only what he sees the Father doing: what the Father does, the Son does.[2]

This is to define the battlefield and to open the battle. From this point on to the end of chapter 8 (excluding chapter 6, which handles another issue altogether) the point of controversy is whether or not Jesus is blasphemously claiming equality with God. In its course the nature of "Sonship" is carefully analysed.

The Father loves the Son and shows him all His works. . . . As the Father raises the dead and gives them life, so the Son gives life to men as He determines. And again, the Father does not judge anyone, but has given full jurisdiction to the Son; it is His will that all should pay the same honour to the Son as to the Father. To deny honour to the Son is to deny it to the Father who sent him.[3]

Two contrasting statements are made here. The Son does only what the Father tells him to do: but the Father has told him to "judge", and therefore he judges. (Conjunctions present notorious difficulty in Scriptural translations: the reader has to note that "again" in v. 22 means "none the less", not "moreover".)

[1] John 5:16–18. [2] John 5:19.
[3] John 5:20–3. I have taken the liberty of capitalising the pronoun referring to the Father for clarity's sake.

There is, then, a sense in which honour should be paid to the Son, and a sense in which it should go past the Son to the Father. To honour the Son is to recognize in what he says and does the authentic words and acts of the Father. This honour is a rational decision based on a disposition of the whole being, itself partly entered into by decision. The particular breach of this duty to "honour the Son" in this case is in inverting the relative status of the Sabbath law and of faith in God. The Sabbath law is precious: it is socially and religiously fortifying to the community. But to suppose that a judgment based on the literal interpretation of the Sabbath law takes precedence over a judgment concerning the love of God is rationally outrageous. Such a position could only be taken up by those whose view of God was a view which Jesus wishes to demolish: that view includes the notion that God is an irrational legislator, making ordinances whose connection with love is merely accidental and intermittent.

Honour to the Son and to the Father

In what sense precisely, then, is the Son (a) different from and (b) subordinate to the Father? The Johannine debates tell us all we need to know, and tell it to us precisely.

The authority the Son has is authority received wholly from the Father.

> If I testify on my own behalf, that testimony does not hold good. There is another who bears witness for me, and I know that his testimony holds.[1]

> He who sent me speaks the truth, and what I heard from him I report to the world.[2]

> I do nothing on my own authority, but in all that I say, I have been taught by the Father.[3]

But on the other hand—

> I have come accredited by my Father, but you have no welcome for me.[4]

[1] John 5:31.   [2] ib. 8:26.   [3] ib. 8:28.   [4] John 5:43.

If anyone is thirsty, let him come to me; whoever believes in me, let him drink.[1]

The dialectic runs on throughout the debate. The authority of Jesus is entirely the Father's: but so far as the world is concerned, He is showing the Father to the world, and must be honoured with a hearing.

All this is where the classic doctrine of the Trinity has its inception: and the rest of that doctrine is built up on the similar utterances of Jesus in chapters 13–17. This is John's way of saying what is said elsewhere: that Jesus wishes in the end to bring men to the Father. But he says it in a totally different key because he is dealing with a different situation. The people with whom Jesus is arguing are followers of conventional religion, learned and devout religion, who have no use for Him, and are thus delivered from that sentimental adoration of which His admirers stood in danger. The sentimental adoration comes through in 5:1–15 and the whole of chapter 6 is devoted to an attack on it: for there what is Jesus saying but that He has come, not to divert people from the real principles of their ancient worship of God, but to make straight the way by which they can approach the God to whom Abraham and Moses were witnesses?[2] But as has become clear, Abraham and Moses can be dethroned from their rightful place in religion by those whose religious profession is corrupted by a defective view of God.[3] Therefore the limitations of Moses and Abraham must be shown: they must not become barriers to men's communion with God. But the chief concern of John is not the adoration of the simple which must be checked and redirected, but the contempt of the learned, which must be answered and refuted. This is why he introduces this strenuous counterpoint between our Lord's dogmatic "I am" statements and his constant insistence on his obedience to the Father.

The counterpoint is brought to a cadence in the final exposi-

[1] ib. 7:38.
[2] See especially on this point T. F. Glasson, *Moses in the Fourth Gospel* (SCM, Studies in Biblical Theology no. 40, 1963).
[3] John 6:19–20; 5:46–7; 8:31–41.

tion of the meaning of "glory" for Jesus in chapter 17. The glorifying of the Son is in his death. After his death he will "go to the Father",[1] already glorified. The glory is in "self-destruction", in becoming, as Paul put it in three words, "Obedient unto death".

But the counterpoint is further worked out by John in his juxtaposition of the expressions "Son of God" and "Son of Man". We have to hold in our hands not only these two, but also the references of Jesus to "my Father". Then we see how between them they keep us clear about the person and place of Jesus in the scheme of our salvation.

Son of God

"Son of God" in John is an expression meaning, more or less, "Messiah", as in Nathanael's confession at 1:49, and Martha's at 11:27, where "Son of God" and "Messiah" ("Christ") come together. In the mouth of Jesus Himself "Son of God" (as at 11:4) comes as near as He does come in John's Gospel to showing a Messianic consciousness.

"Son of Man" becomes an expression used to imply the authority of Jesus over this world. "As Son of Man, he has been given the right to pass judgment."[2] "This food the Son of Man will give you."[3]

"My Father", as we have said, always indicates the subordination of Jesus to His Father's will.

And so the inherent richness of the idea of "Sonship" is put to full use in the Christology of the Gospels. For he who is a son is (a) obedient, and (b) loving his Father, and (c) the heir of his father's goods. These three qualities—obedience, complete love of the Father, and authority given by the Father into the absolute care of the son, are always present in the words and works of Jesus. And this is why in His own speeches, Jesus leaves others to speak of Him as "Christ" or "Messiah", but uses "Son" as his favourite designation of his place and work.

John has one other expression—"Only Son", as in 1:18 and 3:16, when he wishes himself to make a theological statement

[1] ib. 7:33, 16:7, 20:18.   [2] John 5:27.   [3] John 6:27b.

about Christ's place and work. This is outside the reference of the other three senses of sonship, and those, with repetitions two verses away in each case, are the only places where he uses the phrase. (This is to assume that John 3:16–21 is John's comment, not a report of part of our Lord's speech.) And the use of the phrase surely indicates a habit into which the church out of which John came had already fallen: a habit perpetuated later in the classic Creeds.

In the notion of sonship there is, of course, a subsidiary idea—that of *likeness*. But in the Gospels this is undoubtedly secondary to its moral implications. The word "Son" occurs to our Lord and the evangelists as the only possible word partly no doubt because this notion of generation includes a notion of authenticity: it is from a son that one can reliably learn of the nature of the Father. But the vital content of the word is derived not from this physical association but rather from the fact that this is an ideal sonship. If the sonship is less than ideal—if there is, especially, a defect in the relation of love and obedience and confidence—then a son is no reliable guide to his father's nature. It is clear that Jesus never wished His hearers to think of Him as *simply* "God visible"; for unless they understood the relation of obedience, love and confidence that existed between Him and the Father they could not have any reason for trusting His revelation of the Father.

And so, when he said, "My Father and I are one"[1]—a text over which in the days of the building-up of Catholic doctrine there was so much wrangling—he meant not what logic expresses but what language expresses in that phrase: not "we are the same", but "we are distinct, yet as close as two distinct persons can be".[2] It is a greater closeness than any two human

[1] John 10:30.

[2] See e.g. Tertullian Adversus Praxean, IX:

non tamen diversitate alium filium a patre sed distributione, nec divisione alium sed distinctione, quia non sit idem pater et filius, vel modulo alius ab alio.

("The son is other than the Father not by diversity but by distribution, not by division but by distinction, because the Father is not identical with the Son, they even being numerically one and another." Trans. E. Evans).

persons can claim with one another; and it is claimed between Jesus and the Father of all being. But always "The Father is greater than I."[1]

[1] John 14:28.

CHAPTER V

Son of Man

Must We Stop Saying "Father"?

WHEN we wish to describe the relation between Jesus and God, we can now see that there is no more precise expression of comparable brevity that we can use than "sonship". The word implies the personal relation that exists between two people one of whom constantly acknowledges the superiority of the other but is yet given by the other a share of authority. It may well be asked what becomes of such an expression of doctrine if the habit of speaking of God in personal terms is called into question. *Honest to God* does raise such a question. Indeed, it has caused many people to ask whether they may, if they believe its contentions to be valid, any longer call God "Father".

Undoubtedly it was because it had occurred to nobody in the days of Christ's earthly life to question the habit of referring to God in personal terms that the notion of "sonship" was chosen by Jesus as that which would clearly explain what he wanted explained. No more can we doubt that if anybody really wants to teach us that we must no longer think of a personal God, the notion of sonship at once becomes unintelligible: or it becomes a mythological expression which we must discard. So do all such expressions of doctrine that we get from the New Testament—such, for example, as that in which Paul says that it is through the Holy Spirit's operation that we are enabled to say "Abba, Father!".[1]

I hold myself that the position attacked in the opening chapters of *Honest to God* is an unchristian one, and that the author of that book, and those whom he quotes for his authority, are

[1] Romans 8:15.

right to attack it. The teaching called into question is that God's personal-ness is something less than, or at any rate no more than, human personal-ness; so that a man worshipping God as Father is enabled to thrust Him into remoteness, as those false believers did of whom the Psalmist writes that they say, "God hath forgotten: he hideth his face; he will never see it",[1] or again, "How doth God know? Is there knowledge in the Most High?"[2] The moral consequences of this kind of teaching are trenchantly drawn out in the book (and, to be sure, had all its critics read as far as those later chapters their attacks on its theology might well have been less truculent). The simple explanation of this doctrine is that God, to such believers, is a person, but no more than what human language usually means by a person: one who if he is *there* cannot also be *here*; who if he says *this*, according to human formulae, cannot also be saying *that*; and who therefore can ultimately be controlled by the exercise on the human part of personality not much less, and no different in kind, than his own. The teaching of Scripture in regard to God's personality is that God is both infinitely remote and infinitely near. He who taught his disciples to say "Our Father" taught also of the Holy Spirit who would teach us all things: and that same Gospel which brings God so close to Christ in the relation of Fatherhood contains also that which is translated in the New English Bible, "The honest man comes to the light, so that it may be clearly seen that God is in all he does".[3]

The truth then is that when Jesus spoke of God as "His Father" He was not saying all that can be said about God. No man can say it; no man could understand it if Jesus had said it. Jesus said much else which shows other ways in which God approaches man; but His desire to emphasize this relationship between God and Himself, and between God and us, was in a direct line with that reconciling and atoning mission on which he was specifically engaged in the days of his incarnation.

And this truth is much enriched if we examine, in the light of what we have said already, the meaning of the ubiquitous

[1] Psalm 10:11.   [2] Psalm 73:11.   [3] John 3:21.

phrase "Son of Man" in the Gospels. So much has been written of this that I cannot here hope to add anything to the weight of comment that already has been constructed. But the issue of it all for our purposes is quite clear.

"Son of Man" in the OT

"Son of Man" as a phrase of ceremonious import emerges fully grown from the Old Testament, in which it carries primarily the notion of "Man", but secondarily a peculiarly exalted connotation derived from the famous passage in Dan 7:13, where "one like the Son of Man" is seen coming on the clouds of heaven, representing Israel's victory. The dominant theme is still *humanity*: in the general use (as constantly in Ezekiel, when God addresses the prophet) it is an address calling upon a man to be a man—to rise to the full dignity of his humanity. In the special "apocalyptic" sense, in Daniel, the point in the author's mind is a contrast between a human figure and the surrounding figures of the symbolic beasts. The Son of Man here is a man in extraordinary exaltation, not in his ordinary dignity. Linguistically that is all the difference. But the phrase gathered round it Messianic associations from its use in Daniel and in other non-canonical apocalyptic, until in certain contexts its use by Jesus must have been quite unmistakeable. When he used it in answer to Caiaphas's question (Mark 14:62) he was saying plainly, "*This* is Messiahship: *this* is the real victory of Israel." In open reference to the approaching Passion as the centre round which the real liberation will gather, our Lord's use of the phrase is, and must have been at the time, clearly a bringing of the Old Testament and Himself into collision.

"Son of Man" in the New Sense

It is His much more frequent use of the phrase in what seems to be quite another sense that illuminates the point that is here under discussion. He very often uses it of Himself without any openly Messianic intention; and not infrequently He seems to use it also (often allying this sense with the other in the same speaking of the phrase) of mankind. Consider these phrases in Mark:

To convince you that the Son of man has the right on earth to forgive sins. . . . (2:10.)

The Son of Man is sovereign even over the Sabbath. (2:28.)

The Son of Man must undergo great sufferings. . . . (8:31 *and other places mentioned above.*)

He enjoined them not to tell anyone what they had seen until the Son of Man had risen from the dead. (9:9.)

Alas for that man by whom the Son of Man is betrayed. (14:21.)

The Son of Man is betrayed to sinful men. (14:41.)

and these in John:

You shall see heaven wide open, and God's angels ascending and descending upon the Son of Man. (1:51.)

As Son of Man, he has also been given the right to pass judgement. (5:27.)

This food the Son of Man will give you. (6:27.)

Unless you eat the flesh of the Son of Man. . . . (6:53.)

What if you see the Son of Man ascending to the place where he was before? (6:69.)

The Hour has come for the Son of Man to be glorified. (12:23.)

What do you mean by saying the Son of Man must be lifted up? What Son of Man is this? (12:34.)

There are, as everybody knows, dozens more references in Matthew and Luke: but these cover the ground. What have they in common? Why, only this: that the expression is used by our Lord always when He is speaking in an especially oracular fashion: when, if I may use the expression, the trajectory of his speech is particularly high.[1] Bornkamm is surely right when he writes that when Jesus chooses to apply

[1] Anybody who is moved to pursue the implications of this expression may consult my book, *Into a Far Country* (Independent Press, 1962).

this expression to Himself He gives it a new content, but that the old "Messianic" content that earlier literature gave the phrase has not yet entirely spent itself.[1] Some of the occasions in which He uses the words are very probably occasions where the evangelists report His speech in the light of the primitive church's experience; but there are many on which we are able to believe that He did indeed use the expression.[2] And he used it in the context of His hearers' religious experience. By the time of His incarnation, the words had, to be sure, lost much of their original Messianic content. But not all of it. In our Lord's use of them there is therefore just a touch of the "oracular"; but there is a good deal else as well that is new. The phrase "Son of Man", as John Knox says, "stood for an idea, or an image, in the minds of certain ancient Jews";[3] and in as much as they stood for an image, Jesus consistently set himself to reconstruct it. (When our contemporary theologians seek to reconstruct our images, they take their cue from the very highest source). But Jesus was unable—and he surely knew himself to be unable—to use so striking and familiar an expression without being obliged to use some part of the image which it suggested. If the image were *wholly* beside the point, He would have used another expression.

That part of Messiahship (suggested in "Son of Man") which He wished to retain was, perhaps, its sense of authority, liberation, and fulfilment of the people's expectation. That part which he wanted to reject was its sense of a "this worldly" kingdom, a sense of direct victory and of self-exaltation. If "Messiah" anciently suggested a human liberator, and "Son of Man" a figure somewhat super-human, these were ideas in which our Lord showed no interest. They must be transformed. "Liberation" must be understood as liberation from "sin"; and super-humanity simply as no more and no less than what he implied in speaking of God as his Father.

[1] G. Bornkamm, *Jesus of Nazareth*, pp. 176–7.
[2] Mark 9:9, quoted above, is a characteristically "suspect" passage in this sense.
[3] J. Knox., *The Death of Christ*, p. 72.

"Son of Man" and Humanity

We are guarded against looking on "Son of Man" as a claim to super-humanity (in the worldly and accepted sense) by Jesus because of certain passages whose use of it seems to carry a much more outgoing connotation. Bornkamm ends his chapter on the Messianic Question with the conclusion that "no customary or current conception, no title or office which Jewish tradition and expectation held in readiness, serves to authenticate his mission, or exhausts the secrets of his being. . . . The Messianic character of his being is contained *in* his words and deeds and *in* the unmediatedness of his historic appearance."[1] And the Messianic character of his being was to be revealed only in His utter self-giving, in His self-destruction. Now if this is so, what can Jesus have meant by the expressions, "the Son of Man hath power to forgive sins", and, "the Son of Man is Lord of the Sabbath"? Is it in character to suppose that the meaning of these phrases is exhausted by saying that Jesus, as Messiah, is capable of these dominations? Is He saying that His power to forgive sins, and His entitlement to break the letter of the Sabbath law, are signs by which men may see that He is, in His own sense, the Messiah? If He said, as Matthew reports Him, in explaining the parable of the weeds, "The sower of the seed is the Son of Man",[2] did He mean that He, Jesus, uniquely was the sower of the Word? Or was it something more than this? Was Jesus adding this quite new content to the expression "Son of Man"—that humanity in its redeemed state would share His Messiahship, would know the technique of liberation, and would so enter into the confidence of God, the Father of all men, as to be able to forgive sins, to re-draw and re-interpret the traditional religious laws, and to be a sower of truth in the world?

"Son of Man" after all, linguistically means "Man"; and as a ceremonious periphrasis for "man" had the traditional meaning of "Man at his highest", or "Man exalted". The "Son of

[1] op. cit., p. 178.   [2] Matt. 13:37.

Man" figure in Daniel is conspicuous not only because he is
higher than the beasts, but also because he is lower than the
angels: he is *humanity* appearing in an unexpected and astonishing context. The old Messianic belief was very much an implied
protest against the idea of a simple divine intervention, through
angelic or wholly super-human agencies, in human affairs.
"Messiah" is a person "anointed" (that is its meaning) to
some high office and high honour: "Son of Man" makes him
entirely human, though raised by his office above the common
run.

But that which makes the ministry of Jesus a ministry and
not a mere demonstration is His constant emphasis on the
giving of Himself, to the end that men may be reconciled to
God. *All* that He has, He gives. "For even the Son of Man did
not come to be served but to serve, and to surrender his life
as a ransom for many".[1] The surrender of His life is more than
a demonstration of what He will do and suffer for the sake of
His principles: it is more, so much more than, "Though he
slay me, yet will I maintain my innocence before him". The
Son of Man is given—given away—betrayed (all senses of the
same word) into the hands of men. And so, among other things,
"If you forgive men's sins, they stand forgiven".[2] So, if men
are "doing the Father's work" (as in John 5:17), then mankind
will be sovereign over "the Sabbath". The secret is in the
"ransom" text in Mark 10:45. The disciples are permitted to
drink the cup, and be baptized with the baptism—the cup, the
baptism, of self-destruction that will unite them with God the
Father. As to what follows, it is in the Father's hands, and they
must not look to Christ to be the dispenser of rewards. Once
again—Jesus, the Jesus whom they know imperfectly and love
so much with so little understanding, must not stand between
them and their Father. Let them understand that the office
of the Son of Man is to give himself: that is all. Matthew
puts it, if not more authentically, more explicitly: "Whoever
would be first must be the willing slave of all—like the Son
of Man".[3]

1 Mark 10:45.   2 John 30:23.   3 Matt 20:27.

"Son of Man" Is Part of the Self-Giving of Jesus

If we accept this further dimension in the "Son of Man" phrase, we are able to find in the whole "Son of Man" system—in all the places where Jesus uses the expression otherwise than directly quoting Daniel (and need we in the end even exclude those?)—a pattern of the life which humanity is called in Christ to lead. There once again Paul gives us a shorthand expression which every time we use it opens a door on these wide views of Christ's work: "in Christ." Paul never speaks of the "Son of Man", but he constantly talks of men "in Christ", and of the condition of being "in Christ" as a condition of liberation.

Jesus the Messiah is Messiah because he has given Himself, and given Himself into the hands of men. Never once did he work a "sign" in order to establish his superiority over humanity, his otherness than humanity. He rejected this procedure as a temptation of the devil. The devil suggested that if he could show immunity from the conditions that govern human life, he would achieve all that he was looking for: making food for his own use out of stones instead of buying it or gathering it in the fields: throwing Himself from the temple parapet and walking away unharmed: this would impress, but it would impress with *otherness*. It would be taking humanity's admiration, not giving Himself. One might well say that to apply all the "Son of Man" sayings to redeemed humanity as well as to Himself was to demand miracles, to suggest wild impossibilities. That, no doubt, is what the Master wants his disciples to say. It is profoundly difficult, well, it is impossible, with unredeemed terms of reference, to get into the Kingdom of heaven. But the unlimited power which he displayed on certain occasions was really a power conferred on him by reason of his utter obedience to, and joy in, God's commandments and being. No less profoundly different is the life in Christ, the life of confidence in God, from the life outside these things. The difference is like the difference between Christ and the disciples on the boat in the rough sea: which is to say that the difference is like the

Resurrection. There is a sense, a remote and august and mysterious sense, in which Jesus, in saying "Son of Man," was drawing attention to a statement which He might be making of Himself as a pattern, but which He was also making of mankind that had shown faith and accepted faith. "To all who did receive him, . . . he gave the right to become children of God, not born of any human stock, or by the fleshly desire of a human father, but the offspring of God himself. So the Word became flesh. . . ."[1]

This is the central dynamic of the Messiahship of Jesus: the gift of "being children of God"; of enjoying that fellowship with the Father which was His own. No expression that He used concerning His mission to the world can be divorced from it. If it be a matter of moving mountains, then, as in the Psalmist's vivid recollection of the Exodus,[2] where God's power and favour were first made fully clear to ancient Israel, the mountains will be made to "skip like rams".

---

[1] John 1:12–14a. [2] Psalm 114:4.

CHAPTER VI

Divine and Human

"Jesus Is God." Is This Good Doctrine?

THERE is a hymn, written about 1854 by a Roman Catholic author to expound the first three verses of St John's Gospel, which opens with the following verse:

> Jesus is God: the solid earth,
>   The ocean broad and bright,
> The countless stars, like golden dust,
>   That strew the skies at night,
> The wheeling storm, the dreadful fire,
>   The pleasant wholesome air,
> The summer's sun, the winter's frost
>   His own creations were.[1]

It remains in a hymnal that is still in wide use, although it is probably not often sung now. Are its first three words misleading?

"Jesus is God!"—should Christians say that? The question is one which professional theologians do not find much difficulty in answering. Their answer must be that no statement of Christian faith produced in the first five centuries as carrying authority does say it. But the question still gives great trouble to ordinary people, especially to people whose devotion is far in advance of their theological awareness.

What did the early Church say? Nothing in the New Testa-

[1] *Hymns Ancient and Modern* (standard edition) 170; by F. W. Faber.

53

ment urged men to say, "Jesus is God". "Jesus is LORD"—yes: that was the church's earliest battle-cry. Lord—and Lord alone to be sure: but not, precisely, GOD. The New Testament records large claims made by Jesus; but even His enemies did not, as there recorded, accuse Him of more than making Himself out to be "equal with God".

It is impossible to think of Jesus claiming to be identical with His Father. None of His New Testament sayings on the point makes sense if that claim is ascribed to Him. It is our contention, of course, that any such ascription is not an imprecision, but the direct reverse of what Jesus wished us to understand. "My Father and I are one", and "Anyone who has seen me has seen the Father" do not mean that.

The Creed's Formula

Now it was the business of the theologians of the first five centuries to translate into "public language" the theology of the New Testament, and, in controversy, to show where the real truth lay. Those centuries brought out every possible misunderstanding or mis-emphasis that could be applied to the teaching of the New Testament, and on the whole it is held that the teaching of the church, as exemplified in the Creed of Nicaea and the Definition of Chalcedon, states in accurate language what the New Testament means us to understand.

Psychology is no part of the business of such statements. The kind of argument we have been pursuing so far presupposes faith. It treats as settled all manner of questions (such as that of the authority and historic existence of Jesus) which were not necessarily settled in the minds of those whom the creeds and definitions were designed to help, or to keep on the right lines. So we do not hear about Messiahship in the creeds. What we do hear is this:

And in one Lord Jesus Christ,
The only-begotten Son of God,
Begotten of his Father before all worlds,
God of God, Light of Light, very God of very God,
Begotten, not made,
Being of one substance with the Father,
By whom all things were made.[1]

This, as a summary of the Church's teaching about the person
of Christ, comes as near as any such statement can come to
saying "Jesus is God": "Very God of very God" is in apposi-
tion to "Jesus Christ". But does it say in fact, "Jesus is God?"
If so, why does it first say that He is "the only-begotten Son
of God"?

At this point we must move out of the climate of Biblical
study into that of metaphysic and theology, and must ask the
reader's patience while we do so.

The proper understanding of the Creed comes from an
understanding of the precise questions it was designed to
answer. These questions were, historically, put in the form of
"heresies" as often as not: statements by eminent Christians
given with authority which seemed to other Christians to imply
a deviation from the true teaching of Scripture and from the
consensus of the Church. Not infrequently it was eminent
preachers who, expounding the faith to their congregations,
did such things, and attracted enough attention to appear to
those who disagreed with them to be dangerous. It was always
a question of *translation*: of saying in contemporary, sometimes
popular, language what Scripture had taught.

The heresy—the wrong opinion aroused by what seemed to
be deviant preaching—which these clauses of the Creed sought
to answer was the statement that Jesus Christ was "a creature".
In answer to it, the Creed says that He was "not made but
begotten", and adds other expressions to confirm this: "Light

[1] This is the familiar translation of the Creed of Constantinople (381 AD),
representing the original text with one later addition, the words "God of
God". It is popularly, but inaccurately, known as the Nicene Creed.

of Light, very God of very God . . . being of one substance with the Father."

To Say "Jesus Is a Creature" Damages Faith

Now what exactly is the damage done to faith by the belief that Jesus was a creature—that is, an ordinary man with an extraordinary historic task to perform? Consider what manner of faith would arise from this.

It involves at first believing that Jesus lived some part of His life as a man in all respects like other men, with no mission in the world apart from that of being a good man in his station of life. At some point we must believe that He was made conscious of His special mission. It is even possible to believe that He was "adopted" as the Son of God, "elected to Messiahship". Many in early days thought that this was what happened at His baptism. Logically it was possible to push the date of "adoption" back to the very earliest moments of His early life. But at one time or another one must, if one follows the historical record of the Gospels, suppose that this "created man", this ordinary man, was thus "adopted". The name given to this view was "adoptionism", and it was part of the view which Arius, who most prominently was promoting the theory of "creatureship", was committed to.

But what is far more serious is this: that there seems to be no way of explaining in equally impersonal and unmythological language the means by which Jesus gave to *men* the right to become sons of God. Must men hope to imitate Jesus by being "adopted" as well? The only way in which one could explain this is to say that Jesus was "adopted" because of His special suitability for the performance of God's purpose: which must mean his personal goodness: and that personal goodness will therefore make men eligible for the Kingdom. This, however, cannot be made to harmonize with John's teaching about being "born again" in 1:13 and 3:3–5. Had the truth been capable of expression in terms as familiar as "goodness will make men eligible for sonship" there would have been no need for the mysterious words which so outraged Nicodemus.

Adoptionism, and the notion of Christ as a "created man" falls short of being able to show us how the gift of reconciliation is given to us. The truth is so finely balanced that a very little distortion this way or that will upset its whole structure. We must be convinced of Christ's authority, and of His sufficiency for the task: we must be conscious of the need for the task to be done: but we must not be left with any teaching that makes it easy for us to believe that this salvation, this rescue from the bondage of the sin of the world, is reserved only for some, and not available to others. If the Lamb of God takes away the sin of the world, He takes away the sin of the world: He does not take away mine and leave yours. What distinguishes those who enter the Kingdom and those who do not? Only a personal decision, taken in the light of sufficient (though not of complete) evidence. This is what the Gospels teach with absolute clarity. The central Figure then must be one whose authority is absolutely assured, and therefore it must be one whose capacity to do what must be done ("take away the sin of the world") was never in doubt, never hidden. Therefore He cannot have been "adopted", and our entry into His Kingdom is similarly not a matter of adoption, but a matter of our consciously receiving grace.

If a "created man" could have done this, he must command our enormous admiration. He must be something of a prodigy. But he will lose what Jesus clearly most required. For what is it that we should admire in a "created man" who redeemed us? We should admire his personal goodness—the ground of his adoption. We should also admire his sacrifice for us, and our admiration would go with a good deal of pity, and with perhaps not a little shame on our own part. But would he, thus created and then adopted, reconcile us with the Father? Would he not rather leave us fearing the Father as much as we did before, and admiring him for being content to do what he did to save us? Does not adoptionism and the "creature" doctrine tempt us (even though with ingenuity we could avoid the temptation) to go on thinking of an almighty but unfriendly God against whose wrath this champion of ours stood? Adoptionism may be good enough for Job, but it does not say what Jesus was saying.

Now when it was made clear in debate that Arius was wrong in saying that Christ was a creature (and this was in 325, when the real "Nicene Creed", subsequently so much modified, was published) there were some who were but half convinced. Among these were men who said, "We will admit that Jesus had a nature like that of God: but we will not admit that his nature was the same as that of God." Their teaching then said that Jesus was "of like substance" with the Father. Eventually the Creed we know stated that he was "of the same substance as the Father": and the difference between the two Greek words in dispute was one single letter—*iota*.

To Say "*Jesus Is Very Like God*" Damages Faith

What difference does it make if we say "of like substance" or "of the same substance"?

The difference is in a separation of Christ from God at a point where it is essential to establish unity: and the unity must be established *here* in order to insist on a separation at the one point where we must have it.

The Creed insists at all points on the implications of "My Father and I are one": any modification of this through re-writing the phrase as "My Father and I are very closely alike", or as "My Father is one thing, I am a wholly other thing" is to distort the teaching. But the placing of "Very God of Very God", as the second (or third) of two (or three) phrases amplifying "begotten of the Father" shows that the authors of the Creed do not wish us to say simply "Jesus is God"; for that would again confuse the delicate texture of the truth.

The Creed was formed in order to make public sense of doctrines received by faith, and to offer special protection against certain common errors. There are limits to what a public rational paraphrase of truth received through personal revelation can do. But the Creed is misleading only if its dry phrases cannot be clothed with the living truth of revelation in such a way as to make a homogeneous whole. And what the Creed insists on above all things is "begotten, not made".

Who Is God?

Now if we approach the whole scheme from the other end—by asking what precisely is meant by the "God" with whom Jesus is said to be "of one substance", we shall see how carefully the ancient teachers had to guard against the dissemination of doctrines which could only be interpreted mythologically or by an affront to reason.

Let us suppose that this "God" is indeed a superhuman Person "out there"—in the manner which *Honest to God* denounces. Ultimately one can make no sense whatever of saying that Jesus is "of one substance" with him. One could just about make sense of saying that Jesus was "of like substance", or "reminiscent of" such a being. But "of one substance" makes no sense at all.

"Substance" is, of course, not a Biblical word. Scripture speaks of the relation between Jesus and God either in terms of *generation*—which is a figure requiring careful and limited interpretation—or by using such a phrase as "the stamp of God's very being".[1] "Father and Son" has this limitation, that we may not think of a time when the Father was but the Son was not, whereas in ordinary speech the father does take temporal priority. The "stamp" image is more exact, in that it suggests that God's very being is stamped out in a human matrix—humanity being the substance in which the stamp's impression is made. But a too limited view of God the Father constantly raises difficulties about the sonship of Jesus, and unless one is content to paper over intellectual absurdities by the invocation of "mystery" one must look for the flaw in the interpretation given to the truth, however traditional the interpretation may be.

[1] Hebrews 1:3.

But if God is only *partly* to be thought of as a supreme and separated Being, and may *also* be thought of as Being itself, the ground of all being apprehensible and inapprehensible by mortals, then we can quite intelligibly say that Jesus Christ is *of one substance* with *that*. Incidentally we shall also see much more clearly how wholly figurative our language, even our credal language, about Christ really is.

All we must do is admit that our language is figurative. We may accept that the figures are good, that they do express conveniently and briefly fundamental ideas that are true to Scriptures and to experience. But we run astray every time we say "*this* is figuratively true of Christ, but *that* is literally true of Him".

Jesus Does Not Reconcile Us with an Image of God, but with God

We have said much in the preceding pages about Christ's mission of reconciling men to the Father. We must now insist that Christ was not reconciling them to the incompletely revealed God of the Old Testament. He was not (to be more precise) reconciling them to *their image* of the Father. He did not come to make up a quarrel between Israel and a God who was like a husband deserted by a wife; nor to call a truce between Israel and a God who was at war with them; or to pay a debt owed by Israel to a God whose patience they had overdrawn; or to placate a tyrant who was waiting to punish his errant people with death. So many tales have been told about the Atonement, invoking ideas such as "ransom" (unhappily placing too much weight on the *figure* in Mark 10:45) or "payment to the devil", or "a life given in place of ours that was owed", and all these presuppose that Christ was reconciling men to a God whose image they correctly held in their minds. But it was the image itself that must be reconstructed; and especially it was the idea that God (quite justifiably) held the world in contempt that must be exorcized. It was of the devil's implanting: exorcized is the right word.

God with Us

So Jesus is "God among us": and just as we are told in the Gospel that "God loved the world", meaning that God has always loved it, so we are told in His incarnation that it is of the very nature of God to be "among us". It is probably an error to say with too much emphasis that God came among us in Christ for the first time, although for dramatic effect this expression has its uses; but it is permissible only if we really mean by it that in Jesus, God showed quite unmistakeably that it was of His own nature to be among us. "God with us" was a prophetic hope (and to be truthful to Scripture, it was far more of a conscious hope in such a text as Psalm 46:5 than in the familiar passage in Isaiah 7:14), but in the incarnation of Christ it became a present reality—and could be seen, by those who had eyes to see, to have always been the reality.

Eternal Humanity

And it must be to this end that the Creeds, again echoing but not verbally repeating Scripture, insist on the expression, "begotten of his Father before all worlds", and also on saying, "by whom all things were made".[1] The church has always insisted on the eternal existence of Christ, and on his "eternal generation"; not of course meaning to deny full reality to his human birth, but meaning to counteract the error that what Christ showed was something that was happening entirely for the first time. The Old Testament found its way along this road for some distance: the idea behind such a passage as Proverbs 8:22–36 is that while God's creation of the world could be thought of as a finished event (as Genesis 1:1–2, 3 thinks of it), yet God is in a continuing relation of intimacy with His

[1] "By whom all things were made" refers, of course, to Christ, not here to the Father, and a literal translation in modern speech would read "through whom all things came into being". The source is, of course, John 1:3.

creation. There must, in other words, be more to say about
God than that He made everything and saw that it was good,
and now waits to judge of its success in its journey through
time. There is God, who is unfathomably far off, the creator
of all that is. But, said they of those days, there is One with
Him who continually rejoices in His creation. Now, in the New
Testament, we are able to say this far less mythologically. Here
is One who is "God with us": being of one substance with the
Father, being of complete moral intimacy with the Father,
being the Lord, and evidently the Lord, of all creation, He
shows us that God can be, is, and always was, "with us". But
whereas our eyes before were averted from the truth by the
conviction that God could not in any sense be "with us", now
we see that it can be, is and always was so.

We speak here in terms of eternity, and therefore still in
figures. It is no less true that the Incarnation is a critical event,
a pivot of history. It is no less true that what Jesus said was
utterly new. But it was (I can think of no other way of putting
it) no news to God. It was not God changing His mind about
His relation with the world.

What has happened in the Incarnation is, among so much
else, the lifting of the curse which said that man could not see
God and live. That is what man had believed. In his state of
"sin" (assumption, made by decision, of God's hostility) he
must either believe that, and keep his religion at least reverent,
or trivialize God. Other "incarnations" in other religions are
the consequence of heavenly misbehaviour, or some other kind
of error at the highest level: divinities are "sent down" to earth
in an almost academic sense. Religions of remote divinities do
not think the better of their gods for becoming incarnate. But
we are given the astounding revelation that in some sense God
always was incarnate. Apollinarius, who in the end threatened
a disbalance of doctrine, touched a nerve of truth when he
coined the audacious phrase, "the heavenly flesh" of Christ.

It really is true for Christians—it always was true for all men
whatever—that one cannot love God without loving one's
brother also.

We will not, then, say, flatly, "Jesus is God". We will say that Jesus is "God with us", that He is "the Son of God", that He is "of one substance with the Father", and *in that sense* "Very God of very God"—God's authentic truth bodied forth in humanity. And we will go further and say, with the fathers of the Council of Chalcedon (451 AD) that Jesus is wholly human and wholly divine.

CHAPTER VII

Death of God and Death of Man

Christ, then, Is God-and-Man

LET us now recall a quotation from *Honest to God* which we made on our opening pages. "If one has to present the doctrine of the person of Christ as a union of oil and water, then the Early Church made the best possible attempt to do so. . . . But it is not surprising that in popular Christianity the oil and water separated, and that one or the other came to the top."

The Chalcedonian Definition of the two natures in Christ (451 AD) roundly stated, without offering to explain the statement rationally, that Christ is "the Self-same perfect in Godhead, the Self-same perfect in manhood; truly God and truly Man."[1] Controversy had gone on between those who had "allowed one of the two components to come to the top". It continues to do so. Human temperaments tend, being faced with intellectual choices, to turn one way or the other as their predispositions direct them; and to most ordinary Christians a belief in Christ's humanity at the expense of His divinity, or in His divinity at the expense of His humanity, comes naturally.

Here again we have to insist that we are dealing in, as it were, post-Copernican dimensions. One plus One here can equal One —and it is not enough to say, "then you really mean that the divinity and the humanity are aspects of the same thing".

No: that is not what Chalcedon said, and it is not what we must say. There are not in Christ two natures, one alongside the other. It is not the case that sometimes he acted as human, sometimes as divine. He was not compounded of a human

[1] Bindbey and Green, *Decumenical Documents of the Faith* (Methuen 1950), p. 234, thus translates the original Greek.

nature overlaid and blotted out by a divine nature. It is not right to say that there are two ways of looking at Him.

What we may say—the only thing we may say—is that in Him the divine nature and the human nature were "one and indivisible". That is, they were reconciled to the point of such complete fusion that at no point might we say "This was the human Christ acting" or "That was the divine Christ acting". In no other way could Jesus have been "God with us". He might be either "God" or "with us", but, except for this fusion of the two natures, He could not be both. And both He must be; for we may say "Jesus is God" only if we are also saying at the same time "Jesus is Man". (And since we cannot say, although we can sometimes *mean*, two things at the same time, the expression "Jesus is God" is to be avoided).

Two Natures and Not Only in Christ

The principle of Two Natures in Christ is better understood, of course, if we can see it repeated elsewhere in human experience; and in one area of experience this confirmation is indeed given to us. It is possible, and in a parallel sense, to say that there are two natures in Scripture. Scripture is a mode of God's self-revelation to us—through literature acting upon reason and affection. It is equally an error to say that Scripture is simply divine, and to say that it is simply human. Superstition enters if we insist that Scripture is literally God-written: ordinary knowledge tells us that it was written by men. But if we say that Scripture is simply a collection of humanly written documents, then its authority becomes merely artificial, and indeed it is difficult to approach it as having any authority of its own that any other human book does not have. What Christians normally believe, though perhaps it is not normally thus expressed, is that in Scripture there are two natures in fusion: it is divine to exactly the same extent that it is human. No word of it was written otherwise than by fallible human beings: yet no word of it but has a place in the story of our salvation. The temptation often is to say, "This part of Scripture is entirely divine, and requires none of the human approaches to books for its apprehension": and saying this, we make that part of Scripture an incantation which at no point submits to rational apprehension. Perhaps many feel that the 23rd Psalm is like this, or the 53rd chapter of Isaiah: many certainly feel thus about the Gospels. On the other hand, we say of other passages —like the first few chapters of I Chronicles, or most of Leviticus, or Esther, "These are merely human: we need read these only as tolerably accurate records of human activities." But in the experience of the ordinary man—and although when he comes to express his beliefs he often goes astray because of an insufficient command of public language, his beliefs are often a very sound guide in themselves to what the church has succeeded in teaching him—"The Bible" is a perfect mixture of the divine and human. It requires some degree of sophistication to regard it, or part of it, as reduced to mere humanity by criticism: and it requires a certain deliberate advancement in superstition to regard it, or even parts of it, as entirely and purely the oracles of God. We really do believe that there are two natures in Scripture, and that the division of them, or the subordination of one to the other, brings disaster to our receiving of its revelation.

What is "divine" in Scripture is the product of a divine providence only imperfectly understood (as it always is) by those who were its instruments. That providence used the writers, the editors, and the makers of the Canon, spreading its activities, even in respect of the same strand of Scripture, over many generations. Accepted, it becomes the authority which separates canonical from non-canonical, and leaves us with a Book of manageable length which we are content to believe "contains sufficiently all doctrine required for eternal salvation through faith in Jesus Christ".[1]

The truth, again, is finely balanced, and misplaced reverence can do as much harm as negligence in approaching the Scriptures. The amount of acerbity that distinguishes controversies

[1] From the Ordination Service used in Congregational churches at present: *A Book of Public Worship* (1948) p. 201.

based on Scriptural authority is sufficient evidence for the damage that a lack of true balance can do.

Two Natures in the Redeemed

May we perhaps go on to say something bolder—namely that in the "man in Christ" there are two natures? We are never told in Scripture that man, even paradisal man, shared God's nature; but we are told that he was made in God's image: and the word "image" is often used as a description of the relation between Christ and God in the Epistles,[1] and in Romans 8:29 we are given the hope of becoming conformed to the "image" of Christ. "Image" tends to carry the meaning of something inherently invisible made visible, and not to connote anything to do with *substance* or *nature*; but the sharing of any of these properties with God is a condition of close connection, of intimacy, and that is all that these figures are really able to suggest to us, however powerful the associations of the words which provide the figures. Christian thinkers have speculated concerning the effects of sanctification in Christ in conferring on men something divine: as when Irenaeus said, "Because of his measureless love, he became what we are in order that he might make us what he is".[2] It was Christ's purpose that we should be "transfigured into his likeness, from splendour to splendour".[3]

But His purpose was not to make us less human. It was to rescue our humanity from corruption. It is a mistaken (and very common) view of what the church traditionally calls "sainthood" to suppose in it a withdrawal of humanity and replacement of it by divinity. Some passages in Paul tempt us to think thus, such as, "We know that the man we once were is crucified with Christ, for the destruction of the sinful self".[4]

[1] I Cor 11:70; II Cor 4:4; Col 1:15; it is the same Greek word that the Septuagint uses in Gen 1:26.
[2] Irenaeus, *Adversus Haereses* 5 Preface: . . . qui propter immensam suam dilectionem factus est quod sumus nos, uti nos perficeret esse quod est ipse. (Latin translation of lost original).
[3] II Cor 3:18.   [4] Romans 6:6.

But Paul's dramatic language must not throw us off the track. There is a transformation; this new thing—so new that we cannot recognize it as the restoration of a primitive relation, the reconciliation of what God had joined and men had put asunder—involves so profound an operation of spiritual surgery that a death is indeed involved. (It is not only that "death and resurrection" provide the only figure under which we can describe it: when Paul says it feels like a death, and a painful death, he means what he says, precisely.) But it is not in the end a withdrawal of humanity: only a destruction of *self* (yes: Paul says precisely that) which is something quite different.

The Religion of Withdrawal

The "religion" against which the *Honest to God* school has launched so spectacular an attack is precisely a religion which looks for a withdrawal, not a perfection, of humanity. Its best deeds are the least characteristically "human" acts that man can compass. Its prayers are divorced from action. It withdraws from the world. Withdrawal as a temporary expedient is no doubt as necessary as the occasional holiday at the seaside or in the Highlands: but a principle of withdrawal is associated with the notion that the "divine" must overlay and extinguish the "human" in the sanctified man. With men, with the Bible, and with Christ, this is not what the purpose of God has ordered.

All of Christ Died

What then died when Christ died? What dies when a man "dies to sin"? Were both of Christ's natures put to death, or was only His human nature? This is a crucial question, and for a little longer yet we must walk on the razor's edge.

Christian thought has been baffled by this question, and many escapes from it have been sought. Some have said that Jesus did not really die; some have said that it was Simon of Cyrene who was crucified in His place, others that when He was removed from the cross He was not dead, and subsequently escaped from the tomb. Others say that His body died, but not

His spirit. Others again, that it was the human Jesus who died, but not the Son of God.

All we can say here is that these are not the stories that the Scriptures tell us. Unless we believe the Scriptures at this point to be the organ of a conspiracy to delude us all, we must suppose that on the cross the whole of Jesus did indeed die. There was nothing in that event to mitigate death. It has seemed good to the evangelists to record that He said (quoting Psalm 31), "Into thy hands I commend my spirit", and, shortly before (quoting Psalm 22), "My God, my God, why hast thou forsaken me?" If this was not a death, and a death in utter dereliction, is it conceivable that the watchers could have been so misled? We do not have to read back thoughts about the coming resurrection into their thoughts. What they saw was a total failure, a miserable collapse of all earthly hopes. We do not need to pry into the intimacies of our Lord's sufferings: it is what the nascent Church believed that matters here. We need make no mistake about it: it was death of Jesus, and death of Christ. One nature could not die and leave the other alive.

Surely This Death Removes All Hope of Reconciliation?

Well then: what conceivable force could this atrocious event have towards that reconciling of men with God that had been the whole purpose of the incarnation of Jesus? We can find traces in every word and act of His up to this moment of His primary motive, of His interpretation of Messiahship. But would not all who knew Him best, all who stood the best chance of picking up something of the richness of His teaching, say, at Golgotha, "God has killed our friend: we will have no more to do with the God of whom we always expected this kind of thing." It may have been possible by other means to persuade those who received the special graces of our Lord's ministry that God loved the world: but how would *this* do anything but bring down any such dawning hopes to the dust?[1]

[1] The reader may care to turn back at this point and read again Sydney Carter's poem which professes this essay (p. vi)

So often this statement that "He died for us" is announced in Christian contexts without explanation; so often it is treated as settled, almost axiomatic; and to so many it makes such outrageous nonsense that they must either protect themselves by a shell of irrationality, or turn aside from Christian teaching altogether. But the Church has always been convinced that this was the crowning act of atonement, of reconciliation.

Somehow, we are required to come to see that the Word of the Cross to the world is "God loves the world, and always has done". Now let us remember that Jesus, from Caesarea Philippi onwards, had apparently predicted that it would come to this; that the synoptic Gospels say that He only accepted the title of "Messiah" on the lips of his fumbling friend Peter on the understanding that Messiahship would mean this. Let us also remember that the reason given for His execution was blasphemy—claiming equality with God—which had to be translated into sedition—claiming superiority to Caesar—before the sentence could be carried out. If a man makes such claims as Jesus made, he will die for it: that is what Jesus had Himself said. And death was made inevitable by the religious and political constitution of the land in which it all took place.

No, Because It Is the Messiah's Death

But the death was of our Lord's own choosing (John 10:18). It was not a matter of being caught up in the wheels of a political machine. It was a matter of using that machine, running in series with the religious machine, to achieve the end which He constantly had in view.

If I make these claims I shall die for it.

If you make these claims you will die for it.

That is how the pattern seems to build itself up between the act of our Lord's atonement and the act of surrender which He demands of His disciples.

He died because He was held to be claiming equality with God: the truth was that He was claiming obedient intimacy with God, but they thought He was claiming equality. His enemies thought He was asserting a Messianism that gathered round the title "Son of God" in their unusually alert and learned minds. To make the claim of equality was to invite anyhow Jewish punishment, and (as Jesus knew well) in this case the death which Rome could inflict after the translation from blasphemy into sedition had been made. To make the *other* claim, the real claim, was to say what would fall on hardened hearts and deaf ears.[1] It deserved no death, but only thanksgiving: but all the same death is what it would get; death, desolation and discredit.

It was the hard hearts and the deafened ears that made the death inevitable. There is nothing mysterious about that. It was the result of gross misinterpretation, wilful misunderstanding, and of all the animal appetites which drive human beings to consent to these lies in the soul. The encounter between the truth and the world provoked this explosion of malice and grief. And we simply cannot believe that in itself this death did anything but reduce the disciples to blind despair. The Scriptures do not indicate anything else at all. It was part of the design: a part which Jesus foresaw with grave serenity, and His disciples, when they could accept it at all, with horror. But it was not this, as everyone knows, that built up the disciples into a living church.

It would be hazardous to build too much on the special predictions which John gives us in his 16th chapter: there, of course, the pattern that includes the "departure" of Jesus is very carefully outlined. It could have been composed by John in the light of later events, and those who believe so will not wish to argue from it. But the place of the cross in the scheme to which Jesus was committed was that it was the authentication of His constant insistence that Messiahship lay in self-destruction. In Him there was no sinful self to destroy. The sin for which He died, and to which He died[2] was not His. But though sinless He must be involved with sin. He would speak no sin, but sin must speak to Him, and He must hear it out. All of Jesus must die, because preaching the reconciliation of

[1] Matt 13:13–14, quoting Isaiah 6:9–10.   [2] Romans 6:8.

the world to God must bring Him death. He must die because the message is hateful to the world. All of Him, human and divine, must die and know itself to be dying, spared nothing of the agony of death.

His death was an event of "two natures". It was wholly human, brought about by strictly human means and motives, and suffered in a human fashion. It was the end of an earthly life in which He *was God* in self-giving: in which He emptied Himself of all divinity which would spare Him the impact of humanity, and blended with human nature only the divinity which was in self-giving.

Dying with Christ to "Sin"

And if Jesus tells us in that final action that death lies across the path of sanctification just as surely as it lies across the path of physical life, does experience give Him the lie? Does history?

Consider how "sin" had intertwined itself with human history until that moment. From the first disobedience of man (and it matters not how many million years ago one supposes that to have happened) the presupposition of sin, that the author of all reality was man's enemy, placated only by the unmanning of man, had fed on society like a parasite. There was (there is, almost universally) no public and general supposition about man's fundamental needs and actions which is not thus corrupted. The increasing intricacy of human relations and complexities of society served only to increase the stranglehold which "sin" maintained on its ordinances. "Law", which in Paul is indivorcible from sin (and in his sense rightly) was tainted with fear and its actions were the actions of sin, as well as of sinners. Religion, politics and sex were the slaves of such law. (Almost universally they remain so.) To confront a society thoroughly indoctrinated with the principles of "sin" (not of error: there was much righteousness, much justice, much nobility, even much room for grace in it) with the news of reconciliation was to invite that society to alter every presupposition it had ever entertained about religion, politics, and sex. The world had already seen, and Jewry had been affected by, the majestic cultures of Egypt, Persia and Greece, and at this time Jerusalem was subject to the superb organization of the Roman Empire. In the sense that there was not much by now to learn about what man's possibilities were in the fields of government, art, philosophy and religion; "the time was fully come". The parasite of sin had been feeding on all these manifestations of human greatness; what had gone out of gear was already a complex and beautiful machine. To confront *that* with the demand for the adjustment of every detail in that machinery was worse than to confront it with a bid for anarchy or revolution. Nobody escaped the judgment of grace. Death was the only possible end. If at any other period in the past centuries and millennia a Messiah could have preached reconciliation and lived (as conceivably Jonah did at Nineveh), it was not possible now. Truth confronting the world must die.

This Death Is Creative Because It Is the Truth

But it was the truth and it would prevail. A Roman orator had said that, but Jesus insisted on it with His life. *These* may be the human consequences of preaching reconciliation, but *that*—the Resurrection, the coming of the Holy Spirit, and the dispersion of the Gospel through the church—*that* is its further end.

The pattern of human life's sanctification is no other. When speaking of it Jesus tended to talk of death, even of hatred.[1] True, He also spoke of Himself as the bridegroom, the bringer and the principle of joy. But the ears were deaf and the hearts were hard. The world's condition left no other course at all but to inaugurate and follow through a pattern of which He must say, "It is for your good that I am leaving you".[2] The pattern of Messiahship, in self-giving and the preaching of reconciliation, leads through self-destruction.

Hence that which dies in the sanctified man is "the man of sin": the operation of peeling off the parasite is painful and

[1] Mark 13:13; Luke 14:26.   [2] John 16:7.

drastic. The good news is for a season bad news indeed. But when the' restoration is made—and it can take a lifetime and then be but a quarter done—the man is a man of two natures: human and divine. He is not less human: he is not less involved in a world which is a texture of government, religion and sin. But nothing which as a natural man he assumed about these things can escape reconstruction. He has the choice either of killing his own "man of sin", or of killing the bearer of the good news.[1]

The Resurrection—Not Merely a Happy Ending

Until the Resurrection, the friends of Jesus could have no belief in reconciliation. It was that, according to the records, together with the sudden knowledge that God was indeed present among them in the Holy Spirit, that reassured them. They found, as we all know, that their faint belief had now become a dynamic belief. The work was not done; it was only begun, and time and again through later history Christians, especially influential Christians, have spoken and acted as though the Gospel of reconciliation had never been uttered. But the Resurrection showed them plainly that what Christ stood for was inextinguishable, whatever outrages the world might work on Him to show its rejection of His word. Christ was risen. We must say that all of Christ, having died, rose from death. We must not be content to say that His humanity lay dead and done with, that the two natures were now separated. That is to misunderstand again the relation of the two natures in Him. Just as in an important sense "God was always with us", and a humanity was always part of the eternal Christ, so it now remains.

Ascension

And if, according to Bultmann and his school of theologians, the image of the Ascension will no longer suffice to show us the

[1] Heb 6:6—"it is impossible to bring them to repentence; for with their own hands they are crucifying again the Son of God and making mock of his death". (NEB marg.).

truth of what happened next, some other image must be found. It will not do for us simply to dismiss the event because the imagery in which The Acts records it suggests a theory of the universe which science has disproved. What the Church is trying to say in the Ascension story is this: that the earthly work of Jesus being ended, the heavenly nature of Jesus (two natures still) is returning to that place (that state) in which it eternally was. That is why it is a *bodily* Ascension that the old picture shows us. That is why it is a bodily Jesus, with the stigmata raw upon Him, that we hear of in John 20. Liturgical thought on the Ascension always includes the idea of "our going where He has gone before", and of His "constant intercession for us". These are all figures, conveying as best they can the concept that Jesus, eternally Son of God, returned to that condition after the end of His earthly life.

The doctrine of the Ascension has suffered attack because of its apparent presupposition of a "three-floor" universe. The physical details of the picture in The Acts are detail of a picture, no more. But the idea of a three-stage moral universe is not only tenable, but in logic inevitable. Once the notion of "reconciliation" has been mentioned, three conditions are at once admitted: that in which the will of God is done, that in which it is rejected, and that in which there is a promise of reconciliation yet unfulfilled: as it were, a metaphysical projection of the familiar categories "Yes: No: Don't know". This is the merest logic: that certainty implies unity; doubt implies not two but three possible conditions. If then Jesus is supposed to have "come from" that condition in which God's will is perfectly done, and to be exemplifying it in His earthly life, it must somehow be stated that at the end of His earthly life He is not extinguished but restored to the condition which was His before.

This quite apart from the necessity towards which we move from the other implication of reconciliation: namely that in all respect He must destroy Himself. Among these is the necessity for His withdrawal from the world to a condition in which He is not physically present with His followers. They must not, when they are living out the Gospel, gather round a single human figure. They must contain the Holy Spirit.

Glorified Humanity

But in all these processes there must be no denial of humanity, no admission that after all humanity cannot win. "Flesh and blood cannot possess the kingdom of God"[1] wrote Paul: but his use of "flesh" to mean always "unredeemed humanity" explains that sufficiently. Flesh and blood, not a disembodied spirit, does possess it in the resurrection of Jesus.[2] This is not to commend a naif belief in the bodily resurrection of the believer, but to explain that these figures are attempts to symbolize in intelligible language the mysterious truth that Christ's reconciliation of humanity with God is a process which begins and ends on the eternal plane, and is neither confined to His earthly life nor terminated by His earthly death.

And the point here is that these are beliefs which men really want to hold, however crudely the traditional pictures portray them. We need an assurance that God's purpose is an eternal purpose, not a temporary one. We need to know that there is something *absolute* about Christ's promise that mankind may be reconciled, and that there was some certain good to come out of His death. We need to be assured, as the disciples needed it, that the promises in Christ's words and actions were not mere poetry in the end; that when Christ seemed to be Lord of creation He really is that, in consequence of His obedience to and love for Creation's Maker. That, but nothing less than that, is worth a man's dying for.

[1] 1 Cor 15:50.   [2] Luke 24:39.

CHAPTER VIII

"Why Do You Call Me Good?"

False Worship

"IT is as Christ empties himself not of his Godhead, but of himself, of any desire to focus attention on himself, of any craving to be 'on an equality with God',[1] that he reveals God. For it is in making himself nothing, in his utter self-surrender to others in love, that he discloses and lays bare the Ground of man's being in Love".[2] Thus does the Bishop of Woolwich conclude a section of his chapter on Christology. The words express a doctrine towards which we have been leading in the foregoing argument. I should like now to place alongside it a quotation from P. T. Forsyth, which will effectively launch us into our final problem.

This reconciliation, this atonement, means change of relation between God and man—man, mind you, not two or three men, not several groups of men, but man, the human race as one whole. And it is a change of relation from alienation to complete communion—not simply to our peace and confidence, but to reciprocal communion. The grand end of reconciliation is communion. I am pressing that hard. I am pressing it hard here by saying that it is not enough that we should worship God. It is not enough that we should worship a personal God. It is not enough that we should worship and pay homage to a loving God. Nothing short of living, loving, holy, habitual communion between His holy soul and ours can realize at last the end which God achieved in Jesus Christ.[3]

[1] Phil 2:6. [2] J. A. T. Robinson, *Honest to God*, p. 75.
[3] P. T. Forsyth, *The Work of Christ* (1910), ed. Independent Press, 1948, pp. 57–8.

77

"It is not enough that we should worship God." In what sense is it even permissible for us to worship Jesus Christ? An American novelist in a recent book, in the course of a savage portrayal of an over-pietistic minister, writes: "Then Mr Felcon would say, 'Jesus was sad on Sunday when you didn't come to his house. Do you want to make Jesus sad?' and went on from there. I never had the nerve to say that I didn't think Jesus cared one way or the other, but I always wanted to."[1] What comment have we on that?

"Why do you call me good. No one is good, except God alone"[2]: with those words Jesus stopped a zealous enquirer in his tracks. As we have hinted already, the discernment of the honour which Jesus will accept, and the separation of this from what he explicitly rejects, are skills in which the church's apologists are not always distinguished. The danger is always that of reinstating Jesus in the place from which he quite expressly abdicated: treating him, not as the Son of God, our reconciler, but as "a deity".

Jesus the Dictator

It is fatally easy to represent Jesus as a supreme Being who controls our lives, watches us, and demands our homage. It is easy to go back beyond substituting Jesus for the Father whose love He revealed, and in effect to place him where the God of the Old Testament reigned. There is usually a difference in expression, but this difference is apparent rather than real. The Old Testament Jehovah was, we would say, angry, ruthless, liable to judge his people hardly, and only to be placated with sacrifice of living creatures. Jesus is not like this. Jesus turns a sorrowful and tender eye on those who offend Him. Jesus has only to look at you and you will feel miserably guilty. This Jesus does not raise up whirlwinds and scatter the ships of Tarshish: he employs the techniques of the humanitarian father

[1] C. F. Griffin, *The Impermanence of Heroes* (Barrie & Rockliff, 1963) p. 53.
[2] Luke 18:19.

of Edwardian times who does not beat his children but instead says, "You hurt me". Obviously the difference is not a real one. "Jesus was sad when you didn't come to His house on Sunday." That may be a caricature, but it is often the thinking that lies within the more chaste wrappings of common religious speech.

The Uncontexted Christ

The fallacy is here: in extracting "Jesus" from the context that He contrived for His teaching, and directing all possible attention to Him as a divine-human legislator. A loving legislator—too often offering a blackmailing kind of love: but none the less for His tenderness, a legislator. We simply must not extract Him from his context—from the Messianic function of reconciliation.

To be specific: consider a religious argument sometimes used by pacifists (but often used by others in the same general form) —"Can you imagine Jesus pointing a gun at an enemy soldier with intent to shoot him?' The answer to that question is of course "no"; but the argument must stop there. It cannot be inferred from that "no" that no Christian may ever participate in any kind of war. If this conclusion is a correct statement, it must be inferred from other premises. The fallacy is in removing "Jesus" (the supposed seat of authority) from His complete context. That context includes a great deal of teaching about one's duty to one's immediate neighbour, and the special teaching derived from "but I say to you, love your enemies"[1] cannot be taken from its context and used alone for any general purpose. To do this is, by implication, to remove Jesus from His place in history and therefore to deny the real content of His reconciling work. There is no essential difference, except only in the answer "Yes" or "No" to the specific question between this and the situation my father found himself in many years ago. A visiting preacher was assigned to him for a week-end as his guest. After supper my father lit his pipe, as was his habit, and the visitor, a man of weighty piety, asked him, "Do

[1] Matt 5:44.

you think Jesus would have smoked a pipe?" My father's reply
was, "Do you think Jesus would have travelled, as you did, by
train?" No doubt the answer to the first question was "No"
and to the second "Yes"; but both are anachronisms because
they remove Jesus from his historic context and call on him as
though His business was to "judge and arbitrate".[1]

Jesus the Figure of Misery—with a Word about Hymns

Another error consequent upon removing "Jesus" as
authority for human behaviour from his context is the common
one of responding to the Crucifixion with the emotion of pity.
Our response to the Crucifixion should be a complex of
emotions ranging from shame to joy, but pity is specifically
excluded by our Lord's words in Luke 23:27-31. There is
much in popular devotion that encourages this, and our
popular hymns are not without blame here. An emphasis on
the Saviour's physical sufferings is often used by the poets of
devotion to evoke shame in their hearers or singers; but even
some of the best of them insufficiently guard against the human
tendency to divert emotion from shame to pity, and to say not,
"I had a hand in this" but rather, "How wicked were those who
did this to Him". Not only trivialities like "There is a green
hill", but even classics like "*Stabat Mater*" in most English
translations, or "*Attolle Paulum*", need careful watching for
their effect on congregations, and only three verses at most of
"O come and mourn with me awhile" are not tainted with this
emotion.[2] Particularly when such poems are set to highly
emotive tunes, the result can be distressingly far from what our
Lord, in such places as St John 16, seems to be looking for as a
response to his Cross. Indeed, it is far better for congregations
to sing emotionally complex hymns, combining penitence with
adoration even in a heraldic and symbolic way, than to sing
hymns that concentrate, even classically, on the suffering itself.

[1] Expressly forbidden in Luke 12:14.
[2] *Stabat Mater*: *English Hymnal* 115, *Church Hymnary* 99: *Attolle
paulum*: *EH* 103: "O come and mourn": *EH* 111, *CH* 96.

There is involvement of the right kind, that arouses many contradictory emotions, in heraldry such as that of "Sing my tongue the glorious battle" and "The royal banners forward go", or in the wrath and triumph of "Who is this, with garments gory", or, best of all, in the great carols of medieval England that mention the Passion.[1] To extract one familiar and obvious property of the Crucifixion and concentrate on it at the expense of the others is a particularly unhappy form of "uncontexting" Jesus; and it is unfortunately our artists who have much here to answer for. It is even to be questioned whether in our age, when Western Christians at least are peculiarly (even sometimes to the point of exaggeration) sensitive to human suffering, the ancient cult of the Crucifix can be relied on to evoke the response of penitence rather than of pity.

Jesus the Child—with a Word about Liturgy

Another Christian festival which gives opportunity for "uncontexting" Jesus is, of course, Christmas. The very wide acceptance of the cult of the Child among people who otherwise have nothing to do with the Christian way is in its own way evidence that this cult can easily be an escape from truth. Popular forms of Christmas worship nowadays do much to foster the opinion that the Christian Gospel is a matter of sweetness and light. It is worth anybody's while to compare the old colourful liturgies of Christmas with what in most places now passes for a "Festival of Lessons and Carols", with the purpose of noticing how complex a response to the Incarnation was demanded in those former days.[1]

---

[1] See *EH* 94, 95, 96, 108: *CH* 108: *Oxford Book of Carols*, 43, 44, 71.

[2] The *English Hymnal*, at no. 662, gives some hint of the emotional complexity of good liturgical use. The Introit of the First Service on Christmas Day is a quotation from Psalm 2: a context of almost naked anger. The Gradual has as its "verse" the Messianic verse from Psalm 110. The Tract returns to Psalm 2. The Offertory comes from Psalm 96—expectancy and jubilation. The Communion returns to Psalm 110. These Old Testament references anchor the whole of the Eucharistic liturgy

Nobody wants to dissipate the joy of Christmas; but there is a case for saying that the much-denounced commercialization of the festival is no greater profanity than the removal from it of all those strands of thought which are directed to anything except the common rejoicing in a child's birth. It can easily become a mere sentimental drooling over a baby. The error is, again, an "uncontexting" of Jesus. Liturgy, of course, is designed to meet the human truth that you cannot set forth the whole Gospel at any time in an intelligible way. (It was the Puritan error to suppose that you could); but it is also designed to ensure a balanced emotional response to the successive stages in the drama of the Church's Year, and it cannot be too strongly emphasized that liturgical neglectfulness (which is not surely, confined to the non-anglican communions) is a powerful corrosive of good doctrine.

Indeed, it is much to be doubted whether experimental liturgies are of any consequence if they are devised by people

---

down to the earthiness of history, and place the Incarnation in its true context. It is something gained when such a service begins with the words, "Why do the people so furiously rage together?"

When liturgy is abandoned, the first casualty is complexity of response. One idea is kept, the rest are deserted. This can even happen with the much-loved Service of Lessons and Carols. Even there—where in its authentic form a great deal of liturgical richness is preserved (in the actual readings used at King's College, for example), sometimes the aesthetic decorations contribute heavily towards a merely aesthetic view of Christmas.

It became noticeable a few years ago that in the famous service at King's, Cambridge, there was an increasing tendency for the *music* of the carols to conform to a certain pattern. This could be musically expressed by saying that more than three quarters of the service was sung in the same key, (that of, roughly, G major with occasional transpositions). It must be recorded, as a matter of great credit to the authorities in charge of this annual, and rightly much-loved service, that this aesthetic effect has in the last two or three years been entirely dissipated. This has come partly from the choice of music from a wider variety of styles and expressing diversity of mood, but not least from the inspired inclusion in that service of the hymn "Of the Father's heart begotten" (*EH* 613), whose deep tones sound notes and evoke reactions that the Festival must not omit.

who do not fully understand the design of the traditional catholic liturgies. Public worship is the channel through which most people's doctrine is in fact built up; and a lack of balance, a trend of prejudice, in public worship will produce precisely that lack of balance and trend of prejudice in popular religion. Language can be modernized, means of communication modified: but to build on any other foundation than the raw record of human experience and divine reconciliation that the Scriptures afford is to ask for trouble.

Unevangelical Religion

Jesus the lawgiver: Jesus the kind father: Jesus the child: Jesus the young man's hero: these and any other categorizations of Jesus are incentives to bad doctrine, to a misapprehension of the faith. These leave Christians totally unprepared for the assaults of ordinary life on their faith. And all are forms of, as it were, saying "Good Master" in the wrong tone of voice. All must expect the answer—"Why do you call me good?"

The same kind of response must be expected by a certain kind of religion which applies to itself the word "evangelical". A certain very well known evangelist, visiting this country some years ago, included in an address delivered before several thousand people the following sequence, (I quote, of course, from notes taken at the time, and the odd detail may be imprecise). "If you were a prisoner condemned to death, and you heard the news that somebody else, who was innocent, was prepared to die for you, wouldn't that be good news?"

Now the presupposition there was that the Atonement was an atonement entirely of substitution. Therefore the human response to the Atonement is gratitude to one who has taken our place in bearing God's punishment. We need not at all say that this figure has no place in the exposition of the Atonement wrought by Jesus. But the assumption that there is no other figure that expresses it, and no other response appropriate to it, left the preacher vulnerable to a monstrous fallacy. In consequence of that fallacy one might well reply to his rhetorical question, "No! No! It wouldn't be good news. I shouldn't. permit it for a moment. And if I did, I should be paralysed for the rest of my life with a burden of guilt for letting him do it for me."

At any rate I, hearing that sentence, responded thus instantly. What is frightening, however is the suspicion that the preacher would not be in the least shocked by that reaction. He might easily say "That state of guilt is what you ought to be in". Anyhow, he would probably not see my implied point—that to be given by an innocent person such a gift as that he should take my place and die leaves me absolutely under that person's tyranny: a tyranny of memory, but no less a tyranny for that. Possibly the preacher would say, "Yes. His demands are total. You are his slave." And he would justify himself from Scripture.

Now that kind of religion may be a means of grace to some. That is to say, the presentation of Christ's work under those figures may bring some for the first time to take Christ seriously. But about such religion—and there is much of it abroad, even where its promoters are more careful than this preacher was to watch their logic—there is a dangerous selectiveness which is yet another example of the "uncontexting" of Jesus. "Jesus the dictator" is the most sinister of all these caricatures of our Saviour. It is so nearly true, but it is not true. There are many who today in preaching the Gospel are not ashamed of speaking of the "total" or even "totalitarian" demands of Christ. But they should be, if they have any regard for the total picture of Him that the Gospels give. His purpose was not to enslave us, but to bring us into the discipline of God, which is perfect freedom: to offer us a course of duty which is also delight. And if the incarnate Jesus took such pains to redirect towards God any sign of worship that was offered to Him, then we have no right to ascribe any other intention to that ascended Christ whom the Church now worships.

The church does worship Him and honour Him; and its honour is not always of a kind that He would reject. Let the dangers be seen, and they can be avoided. He does not demand of us that which we have no power at all to offer, or that which we have not been given the insight to offer rightly. But how is Jesus rightly honoured?

He is honoured by learning of Him: and this it is especially the duty of the church to make possible when it is dealing with children. Everything possible that can be learned of Jesus should be learned, from Scripture, while the mind is most receptive. Therefore that which draws towards Him the attention of the otherwise ignorant is permissible. And that which induces the imagination to gather itself round the figure of Jesus does Him honour, as they honoured Him who innocently and receptively listened to His word. We must therefore not attempt to displace all imagery, all the hymns which address Him in terms of high reverence, even all the pictorial art which draws our imagination towards Him. But we must be aware of the danger of keeping Jesus in the centre of our thoughts to the exclusion of that possibility of union with the Father which was what He came to open to us.

What is this "union with the Father"? Who (we asked the question a while ago but have not yet found an answer) is the Father?

CHAPTER IX

In the World

The Father Is Now "with Us"

THE Father is not merely a Being "out there". Despite all the ably reasoned attacks that have been made on the "*Honest to God*" doctrine, to my own mind that doctrine stands, even if some of its peripheral ornaments will have to be removed in the end. The redemption which Jesus worked for mankind was not a process of taking mankind out of the world. Exactly what He wanted for mankind is entirely, and quite clearly, set out in the High Priestly Prayer in John 17. In this passage of the Gospel it is made quite clear in what sense the redeemed are to be strangers in the world, and in what sense they are to befriend the world.

I pray for them; I am not praying for the world but for those whom thou hast given me, because they belong to thee.

(Not, of course, "I have no prayer to make for the world", but "I am thinking of my disciples".)

All that is mine is thine, and what is thine is mine; and through them has my glory shone.

(They must now be the instruments of the manifestation of Christ, of Christ's Messiahship, in the world. There will be no others.)

I am to stay no longer in the world, but they are still in the world, and I am on my way to thee.

(In *this* sense God is "out there": there must be a parting from the world, which is the act of His self-destruction).

Holy Father, protect by the power of thy name those whom thou hast given me,

(Protect: then there must be a separation from the

86

world: a defence, a shield against the world's conspiracy to frustrate the Gospel. "The world" is still a sad and unreconciled world. The reconcilers must be equipped to withstand its resentment of their good news: in that sense, they are "separate")—

that thay may be one, as we are one

(—and know what is the secret of reconciliation that is the Gospel.)

When I was with them, I protected by the power of thy name those whom thou hast given me, and kept them safe.

(They were always in danger: but being present with them, Jesus could correct them every time they said or thought such things as Peter said at Caesarea Philippi. They were *in statu pupillari*, disciples. That condition must now come to an end.)

Not one of them is lost except the man who must be lost, for Scripture has to be fulfilled.

(Judas, personifying the principle of loneliness, and rejected reconciliation, has a central place within the intimate circle. In the world perfection even among the disciples is out of the question.)

And now I am coming to thee; but while I am still in the world I speak these words, so that they may have my joy within them in full measure. I have delivered thy word to them, and the world hates them because they are strangers in the world, as I am.

(The newness of the good news makes strangers of those who accept it. There is a clean cut between the disciple's belief and the world's belief. Still separation: still the disciple is "out there": not as Judas was out there, in his own place: and not as Jesus will be "out there" when he has departed from the world; but none the less "out there". Any disciple knows what this means.)

I pray thee not to take them out of the world, but to keep them from the evil one. They are strangers in the world, as I am. Consecrate them by the truth. Thy word is truth.

(But in another sense—"in the world": never parted

from the world: never turning their backs on the world. The world is a sorry world, but God loves it.)

As thou hast sent me into the world, I have sent them into the world, and for their sake I now consecrate myself, that they too may be consecrated by the truth.

(Consecrate: there is the word that contains within itself the tension. "Consecrate" means "separate"; but it also means "separate that there may be reconciliation". The holy thing was separated from the common run. The lamb for sacrifice was taken out of the flock. But it was set aside for a sacrifice which was to bring reconciliation to all the rest of the flock, and the world. The disciples are sent into the world, and consecrated: that is the centre of it.)

Jesus Christ is to be separated from the world, torn away from it: but as His voice carried the more clearly to the crowd when He preached from a boat a few yards out to sea, so His word comes the more clearly to a world from which he is "lifted up". The disciple will similarly be separated from the world, but only so that what he has to say may be heard quite clearly by the world. The separation is moral but, in his case, never physical, and it is never a breach of compassion or reconciliation, because if it were it would frustrate the purpose of the Gospel. If the glory of Christ is to shine through the disciple (John 17:10), then the disciple's work is constantly to be reconciling the world to the Father.

And with God, the author of it all, the same pattern of revelation appears. God is separate from the world in the sense that only one who is separate could love the world: but there are limits to the ways in which we can thus say "separate". If God created the world, God is one thing, the world another. If God has been defied by the world, God is one thing, the world another: but in this second sense, the separation is a condition which it is God's purpose to heal: to that it may be possible to say that the world and God are "one" as Jesus was able to say "My Father and I are one". Still God will be metaphysically one thing and the world another: but they will be morally "one".

The Uncontexted Father

Now perhaps we can see more clearly the limitations of saying that God "out there" is the whole of Christian belief about the Father. In the first sense above, it is only sense to say that God is separate. In the second sense, to insist on the separateness is to acquiesce in a condition which is, on Scriptural evidence, contrary to God's will. It is to "uncontext" God. John 3:21 sheds a flash of light on the conditions of things when a man has accepted Christ's gift of reconciliation: "The honest man comes to the light, so that it may be clearly seen that God is in all he does."

Is it then good doctrine to say that God is *in* the relations between men and one another: that we must look not up but down, not outward but inward, for our relevation of the Father? This is one aspect of the *Honest to God* doctrine which has attracted so much attention. Perhaps it is a fuller expression of doctrine, and less liable to misunderstanding, to say that God is *waiting to be found there*. For what is He waiting? He is waiting for the eye which is "full of light"[1]: that can see what is there, and rightly interpret it. To the eye of unfaith, God is not there: or perhaps He is there only in judgement, only as a force to be avoided, ignored, or placated. It may be going too fast to say that there should be no thought of God as Father "above" or "out there"; most people begin, as the Old Testament begins, from that kind of image. But the only right path to follow from that primitive point is the path which leads through the reconciliation preached by Jesus. We have to find our way from our natural, fear-ridden, primitively reverent belief that God is "out there" to the belief that God can enjoy our close company, and we His.

Anxiety Is the Enemy of Reconciliation

Our natural tendency, implanted by that habitual gravitation towards grievance which is the taint of humanity, is to believe

1 Luke 11:34.

that God does not love us: does not like us. Out of that belief comes all humanistic pessimism. The world is a conspiracy to unman us all, against which we must arm ourselves. This is ordinary experience. Our world today (or in any age) is a texture of human relations many of which are stressful, duties many of which are vexations, conflicting loyalties whose conflict exhausts us. Modern life has its special interpretations of the basic grievance, following which men distort their spirits, and therefore of course their bodies, into conditions that invite coronary thrombosis or slipped vertebrae. Anxiety is the keynote: it always was, but nowadays it is especially evident. Anxiety comes from the conviction that sooner or later "things in general" will best us if we are not constantly vigilant. This has nothing in particular to do with nuclear bombs: fear of nuclear bombs is commonly no more than a fashionable disguise for the basic anxiety. If it were not that, it would be something else. The basic anxiety arises from the settled conviction that the Spirit that Denies, the Father of Lies, the Author of Nonsense and Confusion, is really the arbiter of life; that what cannot be foreseen is hostile to man's being.

A Social Example

Examples are evident enough in western society. The prodigious problems of transport which beset our own country and the United States just now are a direct product of anxiety.

What is the explanation of the obsession of almost all Englishmen with the aim of owning a motor car? Only partly a direct necessity arising from modern conditions. Partly it comes from the fact that a car is a means of free movement and of privacy. Secondary causes contribute, such as the memory which remains of the privations of wartime when not only was crowded transport, which involved an extraordinarily difficult congestion of human relations as well as human bodies, the only means of getting about, but in all other respects as well our tolerance of one another was strained so near breaking point. But a car is a symbol of "being one's own master", of "being in control".[1] You can beat "them" if you have a car. You can also beat "them" if you have a slice of luck on the football pools or at the Bingo club. There is a profound difference between the rich man's search for adventure at Monte Carlo and the wage-earner's "pools" and Bingo. Wages are nowadays so firmly predestined, and the groove so difficult to get out of, that the only way to beat "them" is to gamble in the hope of a large win for a steady, but usually not crippling, input of weekly money.

It is this pervasive attitude to "them"—to some undefined higher power that controls life according to unintelligible principles—that represents popular heathen religion in our age and in all ages. It may manifest itself in contemporary images, but it is essentially primitive. This "Them" makes its power felt through secondary causes—in a crowded modern society principally through our neighbours: in a rustic or savage society through nature, but it is a "them" that does not want to know or be known.

The Gospel Answers Anxiety

Two kinds of Gospel can give, or claim to give, relief from anxiety about "Them". One is the good news that this higher authority is well-disposed to humanity, however unlikely its manifestations in human life make this appear. But that is cold comfort. It hardly amounts to saying more than that "if you don't like what the gods give, you must anyhow be assured that this is what the gods call love". No known religion really does

[1] The connection between a special interest in railways, which in so many ways are the antithesis of the car, and a certain naif but strong religious conviction is well known and easy to observe. The train has a majestic appearance, a sense of authority (missing a train is a curiously affecting disaster for many people), and a sense of predestination: therefore a response of trust is demanded. The 'bus is only to a much modified degree a substitute. Most railway societies have a high proportion of churchgoers, and, for parallel reasons, an extraordinarily high proportion of church musicians, in their numbers.

say this: but oddly enough it is what a good deal of pseudo-Christianity amounts to—especially Christmas Christianity. God is well-disposed, but He will still organize the tornadoes, the volcanic eruptions, and your mother-in-law's quite impossible temperament. The real Gospel says much more than this: it says that the whole concept of "Them" is wrong—is an invention of the devil, and that the Author of all that is, the Originator of Being and the Ground of all being, is, precisely, "with us": not "with us" in the sense of giving His vote for us or cheering us on from the touch-line, but "with us" in the sense of being present *in* those relations which make up life's texture.

"With us", simply *in* the volcanic eruption and your mother-in-law's temperament? No, for to say that would be no advance at all on what we have just called a defective Gospel. Go back to the essential shock with which one hears that God is "with us". That shock is the measure of our presupposition that He is not, and never could be. The presupposition is the root of all the damage. The vexatious temperament is the result of anxiety about everything—about things in general—about Being itself. The dreadful effects of a natural disturbance are the result of man's failure to come to terms with a universe which was made not merely, although so largely, for his comfort and enjoyment. The volcano is not evil because it erupts, nor the tornado because it is a tornado. They are evil when they collide with life and frustrate the happiness of mankind. Man's response is either to find out what causes these things, and take precautions against collision if he can, or fatalistically to say that volcanoes and tornadoes are part of the "Them" system.

Science and the Dissipation of One Form of Anxiety

Anxiety is dissipated partly by knowledge and partly by a decision to treat the whole of Being as a function of love towards man, not of contempt towards him. Therefore the pursuit of knowledge is entirely in line with the reconciling work of Christ. Almost entirely, this pursuit, when it is genuinely scientific, is directed towards the dissipation of anxiety through the dissipation of ignorance. If then modern science is a technique for acquiring knowledge through genuine conversation with Nature (not for imposing dogmas on nature), and if, as Mr John Wren-Lewis seems to be saying, this is a technique that was unknown before what we now call the modern age (that is, the age of scepticism that followed on the "Ages of Faith"), then that same teacher is surely right when he says that modern science is the most Christian manifestation of our time—perhaps of any time up to now. If (and I must accept all this on authority, for of my own knowledge I know virtually nothing of it) the scientist is a person who examines evidence and draws conclusion from experiment, and not a person who having a spiritual dogma seeks to fit natural phenomena into that dogma, then he is holding conversation with Nature, and seeking reconciliation with God as there revealed in the only way in which it can be sought. Therefore any religious formulations which seem to bring the scientific method into contempt, or to exclude it from the notice of Christians, or imply anything about it than that it is a direct response to the will of Christ, ought at once to be denounced as obscurantist. Nobody who has not looked fairly at the methods of modern science, and who has not brought himself to look at it without fear of academic or sentimental contempt, is in a position to denounce the contentions of *Honest to God* as anti-Christian.

But scientific method is not the only manifestation of reconciliation; there is also the other side of the picture. Many scientists who do not claim to be Christians are followers of Christ. (Some who claim to be disciples make something of a mess of their formulations of religion). They often know nothing consciously of any desire for reconciliation with God and their unconsciousness of any such process, or need for it, is no doubt due to the overbearing way in which non-scientific Christians state their doctrines, especially in the popular presentations of the Faith. But it remains true that the response to the Gospel also includes a dissipation of anxiety through a decision to look for the love of God. And there is no other way of making either the comforts or the demands of this "looking for love" become real than to insist that God can be met where the ordinary man is.

The Vulnerability of the Christian Soldier

The command of Christ seems to be that we hate with all our power of hating anything that contradicts his purpose of reconciling mankind to the God who is the author alike of natural things and of personal relations. The training of the Christian Soldier—an image which we especially associate, of course, with writings ascribed to Paul—includes not only a training in defence and attack, but also a training in vulnerability. Ephesians 6:10–16 and Charles Wesley's "Soldiers of Christ, arise" are not a complete prescription for the Christian life. There is also what is implied in Charles Wesley's terrible line—

Deepen the wound thy hands have made.

Many Christians are ineffective in witness through being less capable than they should be of being hurt by outrages upon the reconciling purpose of Christ: by speech which discloses a silly or self-regarding mind: by manifestations of any preference for the unreconciled state. A certain kind of parade of grief, which assumes in God (or in other people) a settled state of unkindness, should hurt him. A certain kind of mental arrogance (discernible often in its effect on the facial muscles) should so hurt him as to arouse in him anger—if it be possible, of course, anger that does not "lead to sin",[1] but none the less a creative wrath that produces an urge to "publish the sinners' Friend". So many of the things casually said by the people one meets are denials of reconciliation, and persuasives to belief in a God who never loved the world: and a time of great crisis brings out the

1 Eph 4:26.

worst of these, if their utterance is the speaker's habit. These should be a crucifixion to the Christian, a nail through his hands. It is, to recall Ephesians again, a mark of the pagan to be "dead to all feeling".[1]

Thus vulnerable, the Christian must also become skilful in the wars, according to the prescriptions of Eph. 6:10–16, if he would survive in spirit. It is a matter of self preservation (but of course, only such as follows self destruction in the vulnerability that must go before). There is a very great need for that kind of clear, analytical thought concerning human relations, psychology and morals, which is implied in the first word of *Honest to God*. The disciple, if he is to be a centre of reconciliation, must be as observant and as eager for the opportunity of initiating reconciliation as he can be. Observance, of course, is the first casualty of the armour-plated and invulnerable Christian (he forgets things, doesn't notice things, and comes to be contemptuous of people who have remained susceptible and impressionable). It may be that the medieval cartography of religious psychology needs re-drawing with the use of modern symbols: but the casuistry and diagrammatic representation of the psychology of sin that the medieval theologians gave us is likely to be found still an excellent guide, and our popular Christian preaching and writing would be the better for a firmer grasp of it.

It comes down to this in the end: is one's conversation the conversation of anxiety or the conversation of reconciliation? The conversation of a God with-us or that of an uncontexted God? It is the first that distinguishes the disciple of the Messiah.

---

[1] Eph. 4:19.

CHAPTER X

Moralities[1]

The Recontexted Christ Is Our Guide

OUR comment on Christian morals consequent on a correct Christology can be quite brief. We have already made at least half of it. Christian moral teaching, we have already said, will be tainted with all the poison of sin if we insist on promulgating it in the form "Would Jesus have done that?" *Honest to God* made some searching comments on traditional moral views, and inevitably what made most impression—and indeed what was most fully dealt with in the book—was our traditional and habitual thinking about sex.

It happens that in this area it is unusually foolish to attempt to say "What would Jesus have done?" The Gospel records tell us that in this region our Lord had no direct experience, and that He said very little about it. The effect of arguing either from His silence or from His celibacy on popular Christian teaching about sex has, of course, been tragic, because the "What would Jesus have done?" argument has so constantly been brought into play, even if only *ex silentio*. What Jesus in fact did was not to be married: and everybody knows how difficult it has been to get away, in Christian contexts, from the idea that therefore marriage is a state of secondary goodness.

We hear from the Gospels on the one hand that Jesus regarded divorce as a lamentable necessity (if Matt 19:8 be a genuine text), and that any such thing was quite incompatible with life in the Kingdom. What exactly He said in this context is not at all certain: but what He meant cannot possibly be

[1] This was written before reading, and without hearing, the Bishop of Woolwich's lectures published as Christian Morals Today (S.C.M., 1964). My reader is urged to read it at once if he has not already done so.

in doubt. He meant in effect, "Alas for the world that such causes of stumbling arise! Come they must, but woe betide the man through whom they come."[1]

On the other hand, Jesus encountered the criticism of the orthodox for not disdaining the company of persons known to be of loose morals; and his attitude to "the woman who was a sinner" in Luke 7:36–50, not to mention the implications of that very much disputed passage in John 8:2–11, suggest that he was wholly at odds with conventional attitudes to sexual derelictions. Therefore the "what would Jesus have said?" argument can be, and has been, made to turn both ways: towards rigorism and towards the condoning of what is commonly thought to be immorality.

What we say on these matters as Christians ought, of course, to be deduced not from isolated sayings or acts of Jesus but from what can be understood of his total purpose—that of reconciling the world to God. This argument might well take the following form.

Sex and Shame

The relation between the sexes is among that whole of human nature and relations which is corrupted by "sin". This corruption is the very first thing that the story in Genesis 3 notices. The association of shame with sex is, to this extent, primeval: and shame is a corruption of reverence. Different religions react in different ways, by exalting shame into religious ecstasy, or by petrifying it into taboo. In one way or another "sex" has to be removed from "the world", where it is simply not safe for it to be. Only in one advanced culture was a really determined effort made to defy the shame which was primevally associated with "nakedness", and that was in Greece, where the naked human body (strictly, the naked male body) was given peculiar honour in social custom and in art (principally sculpture). But with this defiance went as perverse a sexual ethic as any culture has ever had: a degradation of the married state, an open honouring at its expense both of

[1] Matt 18:7.

fornication and of homosexuality. The culture which the Old Testament represents has something which approaches as near to a balanced sexual ethos as any culture could have boasted: the married state was held in peculiar honour, but the movements of sexual love were neither dissociated from it nor hidden away under a cloak of triviality. After all, the *Song of Solomon* was regarded as fit for a place in canonical literature, and as early as Genesis 24 we have something which is astonishingly close to a modern love-story. The relations between Jacob and Rachel in the next generation are constantly regarded as of a different kind from those he had with his other "permitted" consorts. And the frequency of references to the relation between God and mankind under the figure of a marriage (a broken marriage) have already been mentioned in this book and need no further comment. But it is a broken marriage: and the sexual relation is saddened by the taint which runs through all human nature.

What the Greeks were perhaps trying to do, and signally failed in their valiant attempt to do, is sufficiently done in that which is spoken of when the Fourth Gospel says that "the Word became flesh". When Jesus, in that already quoted passage about marriage and divorce said "What God has joined together, man must not separate",[1] he was surely linking the specific question with the overarching principle that the divorce between God and mankind was of man's making, and must be healed.

Eros Rehabilitated

Now the Gospel, in the words and acts of Jesus, is a function primarily of love. And love manifests itself in two forms: one of which can only exist between one person and another person, and the other of which can exist equally and undiminished no matter how many people are its object. Since the vehicle of the Gospel was always, from the beginning, a community, and its object was the whole world, it was the second kind of love

1 Matt 19:7.

which commanded the particular attention of the apostolic writers: and this—but surely *only* this—is why we hear "agapē" so often, and "eros" not at all, in the New Testament. But the *idea* of eros is not really absent from the New Testament: of a love between one person and another which is so consuming of "self" that "the two shall become one flesh". Agapē is clearly what must be predicated of God towards men, and of men towards each other in a community. But the mystical relation of being "in Christ" is better figured by eros: for in it a man and Christ become one spirit, and why not one flesh also?

It is a mistake to say that there is something inauthentic about eros just because the New Testament does not mention the word.[1] This error leads to a very common Christian implication, which one finds in many places where it would not be said that sex is downright sinful: namely, that sex is second-rate. But eros is authentic only if it is an organic relation between two persons, and not more than two. You cannot be "in Christ" and "in" anything else comparable. But to be "in" another person, so that the two become one, is to enjoy a relationship to which the New Testament gives every possible honour.

What is perfectly clear is that Jesus never said anything that compels us to believe that he thought that marriage was an institution primarily for the continuance of the race. What is gained by continuing the race if "sin" prevails? Perhaps His insistence on the indissolubility of the bond of marriage is not inconsistent with, but in a direct line with, his gentleness about the sexual failures of other people because He held that the essential quality of a marriage is that complete and self-giving love which is the best earthly figure of the confidence between a man and God that reconciliation produces. The urge, desire and delight of sex are implanted in man not only that the race may be perpetuated but also that they may learn the last word about a certain kind of relationship. Therefore, perhaps, He

[1] I now want to rewrite that part of *Church Music and Theology* (SCM, 1959) in which I think I may have built too much on the statement that "beauty" is not a New Testament word.

was unwilling to turn a scornful, judicial or angry eye on those whose control of this dynamic urge had been insufficient to keep them on the right path.

That Hundredth Case

It is thoughts such as these that may be behind the controversial passage in Honest to God[1] which says that in an irregular sexual relation "the only intrinsic evil is lack of love". A full sex relation before marriage, it is there implied, is minimally wrong—not *intrinsically* wrong at all—if it can be shown with certainty that the parties to it are quite exclusively "in love with" one another, and that they are already subject to vows of absolute faithfulness such as they will formally take when they are married. The social consequences of such action might well be so serious as to constitute a breech of eros, and with it of agapē: but if there is no such breach, where is the wrong?

That is the "*Honest to God*" position. Can we say that it is the position that the teaching of Jesus leads to?

It is impossible to gather any impression from the Gospels but this: that the Bishop of Woolwich's "hundredth case"— that in which in a formally irregular sexual union there is no intrinsic wrong—would never get from Jesus a judgement implying that this consummation of complete and exclusive love was *in itself* sinful. But two things have to be said in qualification of that.

The first is that if this action be an honouring, and not a defiling, of eros, it may yet be also a breach of agapē. That is to say: can it ever be that such an act between two persons is simply and exclusively "their own business"? Perhaps one must not be dogmatic on that: but on the face of it the unlikelihood is so great as to multiply the odds against the intrinsic rightness of the action very formidably. It is, of course, not enough for a Christian to be able to claim that in his action there is no intrinsic wrong. He must be able to show that there

[1] *Honest to God*, p. 118.

is an intrinsic right. He must—and this is where the *Honest to God* position has most of its strength—be much more careful than he usually is about judging other people's morals. But for himself he must consider whether this isolated action is one in which he really does cut himself off wholly from other human relations, and therefore immunizes himself against breach of agapē. If he does not do that, he "uncontexts" the teaching of Christ, even if up to this point he has rightly interpreted it.

Longer Odds

The second point is this, and it is more important, and, to anybody contemplating qualifying to be the "hundredth case", devastating. It is that although in the eyes of a Christian who understand the reconciling purpose of Christ, Richard Roe may be virtually blameless in his action with a woman to whom he is utterly and irrevocably committed (whose commitment to her will be ratified but in no way increased by a marriage ceremony), if Richard Roe proceeds with his action making confident claim to be the hundredth case, he immediately places himself in mortal danger of corrupting both the act and the relation he thinks it symbolizes. For Christians may have freedom—freedom to say "I understand the mind of Christ":[1] but it is fatal for a Christian to claim it in defiance of the moral teaching of his community. That way lies spiritual arrogance. "It's wrong for most people, but it's right for us" is a thing which a Christian would never say. For being a Christian, he is "in Christ": and that means being "in" one who among other things was "made one with our sinfulness",[2] or as the AV puts it, "was made sin for us". It is characteristic of the Christian, in the freedom that reconciliation gives him, that he does not use that freedom to give himself the advantage over other men any more than Jesus used his "divinity" to turn stones into bread. The same self-emptying that Christ demanded of Himself, he offers to us as the way of love.

This is a sinful and mixed-up world, and in sexual life there

[1] cf. 1 Cor. 2:16.   [2] 2 Cor 5:21.

are hundreds of "hard cases" in any community at any time. There are thousands of lives which have missed much. There are scores of categories within which one can excuse oneself for being a little sensitive, unbalanced, uncompassionate, or dogmatic about sexual sins in general. All these excuses in the end come back to "anxiety", but that does not make them any easier to forego. On the whole, and at the present time, there is still more to do by way of disengaging Christian popular thinking from taboo and fear and shame concerning sex than by way of confirming its attitude of prohibition and censure. We are, as it were, much less than half way to a New Testament public opinion. But in the end it will, one suspects, be found that the secret of sexual morality for a Christian in a world the heathen half of which besmirches sex and the religious half of which suffocates it is to know more than he insists on, and to be free of more than he lays claim to. It matters enormously to a Christian youngster whether he is to feel frustrated, guilty, and miserable in his sex life because what he feels to be fair is denied him: and what his neighbour can do to cheer him up must be done in the name of agapē (for example by making the early years of marriage more tolerable for young people by providing the housing they require). But it matters even more than that, that he should not miss the greatest satisfaction that the Gospel can give him in this life, which is to be able to combine the exclusive, intimate, personal joy of the sexual relation with the inclusive and strictly heavenly joy of the relation of agapē with those around him. Let a Christian claim, snatch at,[1] insist on immediately gaining and holding, everything that Christ has offered him, and he will miss agapē, in the end, altogether.

All that said, it remains true that nothing that intelligent Christians can do to clean up the public mind, and the church mind, on the subject of marriage should be left undone. It should be another nail in the Christian's hands when he sees a marriage, or a courtship, distorted and thrown off the path of joy and truth, by ignorance, by prejudice, by well-meant but

[1] Phil 2:6.

arrogant interference from people outside, by traditions of repulsive taboo, by superstition, and by anxiety. In order to become able to do this, many Christians will certainly need to reconstruct much of their own thinking; and so long as there remains a large and vocal body of Christian opinion which resists this reconstruction, the best marriage guidance will remain in the hands of agnostics. It is a pitiful and terrifying thing, for example, when we see such a manifestation of ecclesiastical obscurantism as that which castigated Professor G. M. Carstairs for including *one sentence* in his Reith Lectures —two sentences at the very most—in which he questioned the rightness of our *alarm* at the widespread tendency of young people towards sexual experiment.[1] A howl of protest at that from the churches made the Reith Lectures, from that point on, a best seller of radio. It was simply protest: not an answer to the question which the lecturer put. (The lecturer did indeed say some unguarded things but it was not these that aroused the emotions of the godly.)

Not Preaching but Conversation

I would not myself say that the proper course for the church is necessarily to engage in a campaign of sexual instruction, or for the local minister to advertize a series of sermons on sex. The difficulty with this subject is always that, in the nature of things, to draw attention to it is to invite an obsession with it. It is the easiest of all subjects to "uncontext" and the most difficult to integrate with the rest of our thinking. It is probably better that the reconstruction be undertaken on the broadest possible front—on a front at least as broad as that drawn up in *Honest to God*. A proper balanced teaching of Christian doctrine will accommodate a balanced teaching about sex. The ultimate sin is a settled state of unreconciledness, a

[1] G. M. Carstairs, *This Island Now* (Hogarth Press, 1963), p. 50: "I believe that we may be quite mistaken in our alarm—at times amounting almost to panic—over young people's sexual experimentation . . . But *is* chastity the supreme moral virtue?"

preference for that state, an insistence on that state. Sexual behaviour is governed not only by the emotions of the parties to it, but by a law of love which is inseparable from man's citizenship of an earthly society and his sonship of God. Where that law of love seems to prescribe a restriction of impulse, we must not say that the impulse is wrong, but we may say that resentment of the law of love is wrong. The law of love is the one constraint which governs the actions of a man who has accepted reconciliation with God. He may have accepted the Gospel in principle, and vowed to live by it, and yet still in a crisis find its law irksome. Then will come the testing moment: will he regard the law of love in the same light that for the unreconciled man illuminated the natural law? In other words, will he say, "Hath God said . . . ?", and allow all the old suspicions to come flooding back. "God does not really want my happiness. God makes regulations to restrict my freedom. God rules, but does not love."

A Useful Analogy from Money

No, it is not so much preaching about sex that will remedy the confusions of our time, as conversation about it. That is—can the church as at present organized so conduct itself, in its worship and its fellowship, that "sex" gradually is seen to be something not separated from religious life but integrated with it? Can that anxiety which is Adam's be deftly replaced by a Christian freedom which involves much courtesy, much reverence, much reticence perhaps, but at the same time removes the shame?

There is no point in taking that further here; but consider a parallel subject which is tainted with shame and undue reticence, and the point will become quite clear. That other subject is money.

It is customary among the kind of people who make up our congregations to regard money as something you do not mention, except occasionally (like sex) trivially. The result is always a quite ghastly gulf between church people's monetary practices in their ordinary lives and their practices in church. The current fashion of "stewardship" is, of course, an effort to preach decent economics in church; and anybody who has had anything to do with it knows one thing for sure: that unless the leaders of a church community can be persuaded to talk quite freely to one another about money—to tell one another what their incomes are without shame or duplicity—no stewardship operation in that community will be worth two straws. The reason why "giving" for church purposes is often so paralytic in its meanness is that "money" has become "uncontexted", just as sex has. The secret, as we read in The Acts, of the social life of the primitive church was "having all things in common": and it is not fanciful to read much more into that than "primitive communism". I verily believe that in that primitive church they were able—even if only in money matters—to talk to one another about anything, without fear of shame or misunderstanding coming in, until the whole principle of double-talking was introduced by Ananias and Sapphira.[1] Money has suffered very much as sex has suffered from the Fall. Both are, to most church people (and *because* they are church people, tragically often) in a sense "dirty". They are so close to one another, money and sex, because both are means of intimately expressing personality. Both are so easily spoiled by the thoughtless and profane.

Nothing so naif or ludicrous as that the elders of the church should begin reformation by discussing their sex-life with one another is intended by this comparison. Money is a function of society, sex a function of two persons who are all in all to one another. The absolute freedom of speech, the "having all things in common" which an eldership should set an example by having with one another in terms of money must be urged only on the couple between whom the sexual relation exists. But marriages often come to grief, or descend to greyness, precisely because there is no thought of "all things in common" between the parties to them. The church will get nowhere by preaching dogmatically to such persons. All it can do, in its

[1] Acts 4:32, 5:6.

corporate life, is *set an example*. And the example it needs to set is the embodiment of reconciliation. Its sacramental life ought to be the very centre of this exemplifying of reconciliation between the Word and the Flesh. If the church's behaviour is in the heavenly sense uninhibited, in the heavenly sense courteous, the right attitude to sex will dawn on its people.

The Church is the Theatre of Reconciliation

To be specific: the church's popular teaching and corporate behaviour in worship is often—perhaps normally—inhibited by a thousand conventions which have nothing to do with the Gospel. There is a quaint tendency in most church-patterns to be selective about the details that are attended to. It is obligatory to follow a certain liturgy, let us say, word by word, but it is not obligatory for the parson to discover what kind of sound his voice makes. The women's meeting on Mondays at three must be absolutely counted on: but there is no real need to ask whether the hymns make tolerable sense. Church life to the ordinary man, unless he is inoculated against noticing such things, is a queer mixture of the inhibited and the eccentric. There are a lot of things you mustn't do in church, and a lot of other things that you could only get away with in church: that is how he sees it. And nobody who see church life that way is going to listen to Christ on so urgent and intimate a subject as sex—or even money. The objective effect of most church services is to make anybody say, "That is a tolerable diversion, but it wouldn't stand the weight of any real concern of mine. It's the last place I should go to if I really wanted a question answered."

When a man knows he wants a question answered about sex or money, his situation is paradisal compared with that of him who does not know it. The church cannot in its corporate life reach people who make no use of its services: but in their individual lives its members can. The great necessity is for our church liturgies—of whatever kind (and neither catholic nor reformed liturgies seem to have advantage one over the other

or special disabilities for this) to be public and dramatic pro-
clamations of the concern of Christ for men. Every detail of
their drama, rhetoric and art should be carefully examined to
see whether or not it frustrates this end. Out of that corporate
worship, which ought to be a mixture of eternal drama and
piercing relevance, there should go people in whose presence
others are at their best, talk freely, share burdens and receive
the comfort of the truth. Persons individually thus become
centres of reconciliation, and thus disciples. And in their
presence, others come to see that this world is their Father's
house, and that the disciplines of that house are more felicitous
than the liberties of paganism.[1]

The "new morality" of Christ is new because, and only
because, it is a function of love, not of resentment. It is
authenticated by that life and teaching in which by destroying
himself he brought us near to the Father. It is God alone who
judges and arbitrates, and God's judgement is spoken through
His providences which form the pattern of every man's life.

But an "uncontexted Christ" will produce "uncontexted
religion": and perhaps in the end it is uncontexted religion
against which the reaction today is so powerful.

When a man comes to the truth of Christianity—when, as
some might wish to say, he is converted—he learns among
other things a strange secret about the Hebrew language.
"Surely goodness and mercy shall follow me all the days of my
life"—thus he sang as a child. But tenses in Hebrew are
chameleon like: they change, as it were, under your eyes. You
can never be quite sure from the form of the word whether it is
speaking of the future or of the past. At any rate, this is what
he says when he has heard the word that the Gospel is charged
with bringing to him: "Surely goodness and mercy have
followed me all the days of my life: and I have been dwelling in
the house of the Lord. . . ." thus with David, and thus also
perhaps, with Jacob: "Surely the Lord was in this place, and I
knew it not."

[1] cf. Psalm 84:10–11.